WAY *of*
Meditation

WAY *of*
Meditation

Christina Feldman

Thorsons

Thorsons
An Imprint of HarperCollins*Publishers*
77–85 Fulham Palace Road
Hammersmith, London W6 8JB
The Thorsons website address is: www.thorsons.com

First published by Thorsons as *Principles of Meditation* 1998
This edition published by Thorsons 2001

3 5 7 9 10 8 6 4 2

© Christina Feldman 1998, 2001

Christina Feldman asserts the moral right to be
identified as the author of this work

A catalogue record for this book
is available from the British Library

ISBN 0 00 711684 5

Printed and bound in Great Britain by
Martins the Printers Limited, Berwick upon Tweed

This book is dedicated to all of my teachers who have been living examples of the path of wisdom and compassion.

To Sara and Arran, always an inspiration.

Contents

Introduction

For anyone wishing to explore meditation there has never been a richer time to do so. Meditation is no longer the territory of cloistered, religious communities but is readily available to all, regardless of background or religious affiliation. Meditation practices are no longer considered esoteric techniques, shrouded in secrecy but are increasingly being integrated into every level of our culture. Meditation has become the path of countless people who seek spiritual renewal, well-being, calmness and an enriched quality of life. The escalating busyness, noise and stress of our world compels many of us to turn inwardly to find a refuge of stillness and understanding.

The purpose of meditation is to transform and awaken us. It is intended to bring about change – through understanding, compassion and clarity of seeing. Through meditation practice our way of seeing ourselves – our minds, bodies, characters – alters through a process of becoming increasingly sensitive and aware. Our minds have greater access to calmness and clarity, our ways of perceiving ourselves become more intuitive and direct and we begin to understand ourselves with greater depth and compassion. We learn the art of simplicity and disentangling ourselves from the knots of confusion, images, habitual reactions and tension. We learn the skills of calmness and discover a way to be at peace with ourselves. The personal transformation that occurs translates into a growing capacity to approach our lives with increasing skillfulness, wisdom and care. The choices we make in our lives, our way of relating to other people and the events of our lives, is guided by sensitivity, mindfulness and calm.

Within the variety of schools of meditation there are both mystical and practical elements. Through meditation practice we open up to new understandings and revelations, we enter into previously unfamiliar territory of stillness, oneness and grace. Profound and sometimes startling encounters with depths of concentration, peace and unity are possible through meditation practice. The insights that come to us through meditation translate into very real changes in our lives. Our minds and bodies calm – a tangible sense of well-being and balance begins to permeate all of our lives. Our capacity to think clearly and intuitively deepens, our potential for creativity is enhanced and the inner calmness we discover manifests in an increased calmness and harmony in our lives.

Meditation is inherently experiential. It cannot be learned as a purely scholastic subject nor simply taught as an intellectual exercise. Meditation is not a new belief system to be adopted nor a collection of information to be absorbed. Whatever style or discipline we adopt its effectiveness is reliant upon our direct personal exploration, practice and experience with it. Meditation introduces us to the life of our mind, body and feelings – on a moment to moment level we increasingly see clearly the ways we affect our world and the ways we are affected by it. This is the starting point of a journey of transformation – the possibility of travelling new pathways in our lives and relationships emerges. There are thousands of meditation styles and practices in existence which each have unique differences and fundamental similarities. The primary theme that is shared within this variety of disciplines is the invitation to direct and personal experience. No one can substitute for us on this journey, no one can give to us the profound benefits of meditation, no one can effect change for us – every tradition of meditation invites us to participate directly and to see for ourselves.

Throughout history people have retreated to mountain tops, to deserts and caves in order to meditate; to find an inner sanctuary of calmness, depth and wisdom. Every culture and tradition in our world, from Asia to the Amazon, has created within it a system or discipline designed to evoke altered states of consciousness, an enhanced sense of the sacred and to bring to fruition our own potential for awakening. Meditation is not a mindless repetition of a ritual or formula but a direct response to our own aspirations for oneness, wisdom and freedom. As meditation has become more accessible in recent decades there is no longer the demand to withdraw from the world or profess life-long vows. We learn to cultivate a path of peace and understanding in the midst of our lives with their variety of demands and challenges guided by the same longings for calm, depth and wisdom.

Before we ever begin formally to practise meditation we will all experience both the longings for peace and depth and glimpses of genuine meditation. Moments when our minds calm and still: maybe a moment walking through a park when our attention is captivated by the sound of a bird and we listen wholeheartedly; it may be a moment when we feel deeply touched by the sorrow or pain of a friend, and separation gives way to deep intimacy and openheartedness; or perhaps the at times surprising moments within ourselves when we are able to let go of anxiety and preoccupation and experience hints of oneness and clarity – these are moments of meditative experience. These moments, as well as the vast variety of meditative practices and systems are like 'the finger pointing at the moon' – in moments of stillness and calm we have just a brief glimpse of the richness and harmony possible for us; the challenge of developing and sustaining a path still lies before us. They invite us to discover for ourselves the heart of meditation. These moments inspire us to discover and develop an enduring peace, happiness and stillness, rather than the random moments previously encountered.

Through this book I will attempt to describe some of the major paths of meditation, looking at both their unique features and aims, and the essential principles they share. There are basic instructions describing the ways to begin to practise paths of concentration, devotion and mindfulness. The chapter on calming the mind and body provides some simple techniques for alleviating stress and tension. Exercises for integrating formal meditation into our daily lives are given.

This book will provide the essential information that will enable anyone to begin a path of meditation and to experience its benefits directly. It is an invitation for each of us to discover new dimensions of well-being, calm and understanding.

ONE

PRINCIPLES OF
Meditation

What is meditation? As we begin to explore this question for ourselves we are faced with the fact that there are hundreds of schools
and systems of meditation that include concentration, devotion,
visualization, mindfulness and a variety of other ways to calm and
focus the mind. Within this diversity of paths there are genuine differences in emphasis and practice yet beneath this apparent vari-
ance there are core elements and parallel principles found in all
traditions. At the most fundamental level all traditions are concerned with a process of transforming our consciousness. Within
the variety of styles the themes of happiness, compassion, simplicity, calmness and depth are repeated, only in different words. Every
tradition will highlight the deepening in acceptance, patience, ethics
and wisdom. Different temperaments will be drawn to different
styles of meditation practice or specific spiritual disciplines, yet
every system will ask the practitioner to foster the essential principles of meditation shared by all traditions. It is the development of
these core principles, rather than the comparison of the differences,
that allows the deepening of meditation. Some of these essential
and shared principles I would like to highlight.

Core Principles

There are several core principles which run through all meditative
disciplines. Attention, awareness, understanding and compassion
form the basic skeleton of all systems of meditation. Attention is the
means of establishing ourselves in the present moment, providing
focus and simplicity. There are hundreds of ways to cultivate attentiveness that share the essential direction of developing clarity,
balance and calm. Awareness is a fundamental direction in all
meditation. Developing and establishing a consciousness that is light,
unburdened, sensitive and clear provides an inner environment that

is intuitive and still. Clear and profound understanding is the direction of all meditation. Understanding is born of the direct and immediate perception of our inner and outer worlds. Understanding the forces that move us in our actions, speech, relationships and beliefs provides the possibility of travelling new pathways in our lives and is part of the tapestry of deepening wisdom. Understanding the processes that shape and create our inner and outer world forms part of the pathway of wisdom. The vast range of meditative traditions agree that it is understanding that frees us. Compassion is a fundamental principle of meditation. Meditation is not a narcissistic, self-interested path. It provides the foundation for love, integrity, compassion, respect and sensitivity.

The array of different schools will develop these core principles which will be discussed in greater detail in the following chapters. The differences in the pathways of meditation that have evolved are primarily shaped through the differing emphasis that is given to one of the core principles over others; all pathways will include the full range of these principles to differing degrees. Equally the differing schools of meditation will emphasize the significance of establishing a strong foundation for meditation to develop.

Foundations of Meditation

Happiness

The myriad paths of meditation find agreement not only in the ingredients of their development but equally in their objectives. The search for genuine happiness and peace are core elements both in meditation and in our lives. Beset by the whole range of human maladies and struggles – loss, disappointment, tension, illness and

3

confusion, we search for a way to end sorrow and conflict. In our lives we seek an enduring happiness and peace, deeper than just the temporary gratification of our passing wants and appetites. We look for ways for our hearts to sing with joy, delight and appreciation. Struggling with anger, tension, restlessness, meaninglessness or fear we search for ways to be at peace with ourselves and others, to live with calmness and depth.

Frequently in our lives we have attempted to find solutions to these conflicts and find happiness through avoiding challenging situations or endeavouring to create a 'perfect' world for ourselves where there is an absence of the disturbing, challenging or unpleasant. Or we endlessly endeavour to find happiness and peace through attempting to satisfy every desire that arises – more things, more achievements, more experiences. We begin to look at this longing for happiness and peace in new ways as we awaken to the fact that no matter how controlled or armoured our life is the world will always bring us more changes, new circumstances and challenges that we cannot avoid or control. We realize that there is a difference between pleasure and happiness and there is not enough of any-thing in the world that can be possessed or gained that can provide the happiness and peace we search for. No matter how much we gain or acquire we are not exempt from the possibility of loss. Our lives will always be a blend of the delightful and the challenging, the pleasant and the unpleasant, flattering and disturbing encounters, health and sickness. Endeavours to control the unpredictable and uncertain elements in life leaves us fearful and tense. Living in fan-tasies or ideals of how life 'should be' is a rejection of reality that banishes us from calm and balance. We begin to discover that avoidance, control and fantasy are not pathways to happiness but to confusion and conflict.

These primary insights are turning points in ourselves and are the beginning of meditation. They lead us not to dismiss or reject the world around us or belabour ourselves with judgement or despair, but to begin to look within ourselves for the source of happiness and the ways to foster it. We realize that to bring change in our personal lives and our world we will need to bring about radical change within our own hearts and minds. We begin to look not only for a genuine way to happiness but also cultivate the willingness to understand the dynamics of unhappiness and discontent. We begin to question our prejudices, opinions and beliefs and understand the way in which they can blind us to understanding what is true in the circumstances and events we meet. Instead of avoiding conflict or projecting blame in the face of disturbance, we find new encouragement to explore the nature of conflict, anger, fear and resentment and begin to understand the relationship between distress and its cause. Instead of searching the world for satisfaction, gratification and relief from restlessness and tension we become increasingly attentive to our inner life, and there are glimmers of sensitivity and understanding. Rather than turning on the television in an attempt to distance ourselves from anxiety or distress we learn to explore and untangle those feelings. Rather than being lost in anger and resistance to someone who disturbs us we find the calm and willingness to stay present and begin to understand the nature of our conflict.

With a greater willingness to be consciously present and awake in each moment, rather than being lost in struggle or resistance, our minds begin to calm and there emerges a deeper sense of harmony and rapport within ourselves and with the world. We discover that peace is not the elimination of the disturbing or challenging but the capacity to meet the changing circumstances of our lives with balance and understanding. We begin to sense a profound happiness

5

that is not reliant upon a 'perfect' world, but that stems from the clarity, calmness and contentment of our own minds and hearts. It is not the happiness of exhilaration or excitement but an enduring happiness born of sensitivity, balance and appreciation.

The Path

All traditions will portray meditation as a path, a living dynamic process of unfoldment. It is intended to take us from confusion to clarity, from entanglement to freedom, from discontent to happiness, from agitation to serenity. The practice of meditation will not insulate us from the pain that our lives may bring, nor is it an escape from the challenges we will all be asked to address in our lives. It will enable us to meet all of the variety of changes and challenges of our life with increasingly deep levels of acceptance, balance, understanding and compassion. Meditation is not a path of passivity or withdrawal; it will empower and free us to live with greater skilfulness, vitality and intuition. Through meditation we find the inner skills and resources that enable greater responsiveness and clarity in life.

Meditation is not a magical solution nor will the different schools of meditation dispense prescriptions and formulae to impose upon the changing events we encounter. There is no system of meditation that will guarantee a quick and painless solution to the variety of dilemmas we meet in our lives. As a path of change and transformation all traditions of meditation will ask us to be a conscious participant in the development of the discipline we adopt and in the process of meditation. An integral aspect of all meditative paths lies in their practice and application. We are not passengers but travellers. There are qualities of heart and mind that we will need to foster and develop and other qualities we will be asked to understand

and let go of. One of the meditation principles that runs through the variety of spiritual disciplines is the emphasis that is given to laying firm and clear foundations for the development of a meditative practice.

Ethics

Every meditative tradition will emphasize the need to establish a basis for meditation upon the foundation of a moral or ethical life that fosters a mind and heart of mindfulness, compassion and sensitivity. The precepts, vows and commandments of the various traditions are not intended to be rules blindly adhered to but instead highlight the integral link between an ethical life and a mind that is able to deepen in calm and understanding. If in our lives we are engaged in actions, speech, lifestyles or pursuits that bring harm or pain to ourselves or to others, it is exceedingly difficult for the mind to deepen in serenity or compassion. Instead through unethical action or speech that harms ourselves or others, the mind collects residues of regret, guilt and unease. These feelings in turn create endless streams of thought and agitation preventing inner calmness and depth. Engagement in unethical action or speech fosters a pronounced sense of disharmony and fear, anger and alienation. For example, a cosmetics company, aware of the high turnover rate among the technicians involved in testing products on animals, invited an instructor to teach meditation as a stress reduction technique. Paradoxically, the experiment ended with many of the staff resigning as they connected with their intrinsic unease about the nature of their work. The discovery of the happiness so integral to meditation rests upon the harmony and clarity we cultivate in our lives and relationships, both inwardly and outwardly through our actions, speech, thoughts and choices.

Meditation is not ethically neutral nor is it solely a path of inner transformation intent upon achieving exotic states of inner experience. It is directed towards not only the cultivation of calm and wisdom, but also compassion, sensitivity, forgiveness, love and generosity. Meditation is a path not only of inner change, but a path that enables us to touch our relationships and the world around us with compassion, care and peace. It is not possible to separate the quality of our meditation from the quality of our lives. If our lives are saturated with tension, conflict or remorse this will be reflected in our meditation. If the culture of our lives and relationships is based upon peace, understanding and sensitivity, this too will be reflected in our meditation.

The ethical guidelines of any tradition show us the way to a life of harmony and peace and are the vehicles for embodying the spirit of meditation in every circumstance and moment of our lives. They show us the way to live a life of harmlessness, tolerance and compassion. Giving attention to the truthfulness of our speech, cultivating honesty, showing reverence for life through non-harming, bringing integrity and respect into our relationships with other people and fostering a mind and body that is unclouded by intoxicants – these are the ingredients of a life of peace and a mind that is easily collected and focused in meditation.

Attitude

Right attitude is one of the essential principles of meditation practice in all traditions. Most styles of meditation are simple but this does not imply that they are easy. Our approach to any style of meditation is significant and profoundly influences the way in which our experience will unfold. The willingness to learn, the humility to accept the moments we falter, the inspiration to begin again in every moment are all fundamental ingredients of right attitude. Right attitude is the willingness to bring profound patience, openness and acceptance to our path. Every moment is greeted as our teacher, including the moments of boredom, restlessness and resistance. We learn to welcome even the sometimes painful discoveries of our own frailties and prejudices as invitations to deepen in understanding. The path cannot be separated from the goal in meditation. If we seek peace then we need to develop our path in a peaceful way – judgement, striving and forcing are not conducive to peace. If we seek compassion then compassion must be an integral part of our own approach to meditation – intolerance, blame and rejection are not elements of compassion. If we seek calm, excessive ambitiousness and preoccupation with goals are not appropriate or conducive.

Many people come to meditation practice inspired by the stories of great saints and mystics who have been changed through profound spiritual experiences and altered states of consciousness. We may find ourselves looking to meditation as a fast track to our own transcendental experiences and breakthroughs. Investing too much in these expectations we may easily feel disappointed or disillusioned when our initial experiences seem to fall far short of our ideals. Vision and inspiration are a vital ingredient in developing our meditation practice, but these need to be finely balanced with a number of other qualities of heart and mind that allow us to become clearly established in the reality of the present moment with balance and openness. All meditative traditions are paths from here to there, a way of realizing the understanding and compassion that is possible for all of us. For us to fulfil those possibilities, to realize our vision and aspiration we need to begin with the 'here', to connect clearly and fully with the truth of our experience in this moment with an attitude of acceptance and balance.

9

You do not need to be a spiritual expert, religiously educated or belong to a particular tradition in order to meditate. For those who are just beginning a path and for those who have had vast previous experience in meditation, one simple yet primary ingredient is shared. It is the willingness to learn, to see clearly, to be whole-hearted in our path. Meditation is essentially a 'present' moment experience and exploration. There are goals, directions and aspirations yet our practice of meditation and attention is focused upon the moment we are in and not upon the promises and ideals of the future. Whatever is occurring in this moment is the grist for and the birthplace of understanding, calm and peace.

Patience

When you practise meditation and discover a mind that seems to be bursting with thoughts, a body that is restless or uncomfortable and emotions that are unpredictable or overwhelming it is easy to conclude that your meditation is impossible and worthless. The moment you focus your attention it seems to be swept away by memories from the past, planning the future or lost in the apparently endless mind storms of the present. You may be tempted to think that your meditation can only truly begin once you have succeeded in getting rid of or overcoming all of the distractions that plague you. This is a conclusion and an attitude that can only lead to tension, struggle and further confusion as you struggle with the apparently bottomless well of distractions. Consenting to this attitude breeds forcing, willpower and striving but does not lead to peace, calmness or understanding.

Patience is one of the primary enabling principles of meditation practice. It is the quality that allows us to find calmness and harmony in every moment rather than the struggle and tension born of impatience. The preoccupations, thoughts and distractions that appear to plague us and prevent us from meditating are not obstacles to be overcome or enemies to struggle with. It is in the midst of all of these that we learn some of the deepest lessons of our lives and our meditation. It is easy to hold love, compassion, acceptance and simplicity as ideals to be achieved in the future. It is also true that anyone can be compassionate when they remain unchallenged, we can love easily when surrounded by flattery, we can easily be calm when we are undisturbed – but this is not the truth of our lives. It is in the midst of disturbance, challenge and the difficult that we learn most deeply about acceptance, balance and compassion. The willingness to let go of our comparisons, evaluations and preoccupations with goals is a major factor in cultivating patience, to stay steady and balanced in the midst of busyness and confusion.

As we are faced with the variety of forces of our minds, hearts and bodies that appear to pull us away from our meditation it is patience that enables us to return over and over to the moment we are in with calmness and ease. No matter how lost we become in our thoughts and preoccupations, we can begin again to cultivate awareness and connectedness in the very next moment. The willingness to begin anew in every moment, free from judgement or conclusion is always possible for us. It is the embodiment of patience.

Acceptance

The capacity for acceptance is another of the primary principles that allows meditation to deepen and that runs through the variety of approaches. True acceptance is neither blind nor passive, but the capacity to see things as they actually are, free from judgement or prejudice. Acceptance is the extension of generosity, tolerance and forgiveness.

11

The process of inner change includes the process of becoming increasingly aware and sensitive to our inner landscape. In cultivating the power of attention we are revealed to ourselves. The variety of inner processes and dynamics that shape the life of our hearts and minds becomes progressively more visible to us. No one has yet created a path of meditation in which we are able to bypass ourselves – our bodies, emotions, minds, or personalities on the way to enlightenment, peace and understanding. Instead through meditation we become increasingly intimate with all the variety of thoughts, feelings, impressions and aspirations that shape us as human beings. We do not always enjoy or appreciate facets of our being that are revealed through our meditation practice. Qualities such as greed, anger, jealousy or indifference are not easy to accept with kindness and tolerance. It is easy to become judgmental and rejecting of parts of ourselves that we dislike because they are not in accord with our image of who we think we should be. Our judgements and rejections serve only to harden the mind and create endless agitation as we endeavour to avoid what we condemn within ourselves.

In a very real way meditation begins with acceptance. It allows us to soften and open, to bring compassion and generosity of heart. We do not have to justify, excuse or villify the variety of thoughts and feelings that arise. As we become increasingly aware and sensitive to the movements of our minds and hearts we also more deeply understand that rarely do they come to us through personal choice or selection but are born of confusion and misunderstanding. We are not always in control of our minds and hearts – this is a significant understanding. Rarely do we wake in the morning and decide it is a good day to be depressed or angry. Equally it is not so simple for us to wake in the morning and decide it's a timely day to be happy or compassionate. Understanding with sensitivity and balance the unpredictable nature of our thoughts and feelings enables us to step back just a little, to refrain from judgement, to see things as they actually are and to stay balanced. This is the embodiment of acceptance and compassion.

Acceptance is the withdrawal of judgement and prejudice; this is also the beginning of change and transformation. Instead of resigning ourselves to helplessness or despair in the face of our thoughts and feelings or resisting them with tension and struggle we can turn our attention to meet directly whatever thoughts or feelings are present without conditions. Surrounding those inner processes with a clear and balanced attentiveness creates a relationship of interest and exploration rather than rejection. We begin to sense the possibility of new pathways of understanding, letting go and depth.

Simplicity

Simplicity is a fundamental principle of meditation found in all spiritual traditions. Cultivating simplicity is in the service of establishing an environment of calmness and wholeheartedness in our lives and within ourselves. There are many dimensions to simplicity. Simplicity does not imply abandoning our lives, work and relationships. Simplicity is concerned with our approach to all of these areas of our life. Conscious simplicity is a path of disentangling ourselves from complexity, excess and the confusion generated by a mind that is fragmented and scattered. Excess may be in terms of possessions, commitments or thought. The mind that is burdened by excess in any area, is a mind that is starved of calmness and balance. Alienated from inner calm we are prone to habitual reactions and feelings of being overwhelmed by the events of our inner and outer world. Cultivating a path of simplicity begins with the honest reflection upon our lives to see where there is excessive complexity and entanglement. Do we do too much? Are we overcommitted? Do we want too much? These areas signal their presence through tension, obsessive or repetitive thinking, hab-itual reactions and stress. We can interpret these signals of complexity and excess as messengers that invite us to give clear and conscious attention to the ways we may be able to cultivate disentanglement, simplicity and calm.

Simplicity is a path that is consciously developed through calm attention and wholeheartedness. Learning to be simply present, attending wholeheartedly to the moment we are in, is the path of meditation that can be applied to the whole of our lives. The culti-vation of simplicity invariably has with it the companion of renun-ciation – not in the pursuit of asceticism but in the service of calmness and balance. Layers of judgement, evaluation and com-parison are unnecessary burdens that distort our capacity to see each moment and each person in our lives as it actually is. We can learn to let go, to bring a fullness of attention to one moment at a time. In any moment of our lives it is not possible to attend to or solve every detail of our past or future. It is only possible to fully attend to and care for the moment we are in. Thoughts of past and future will continue to arise in the present – held in the light of clear and simple attentiveness they are divested of their urgency and will also pass. Held in the light of clear attentiveness there is the possi-bility of a more intuitive response emerging.

Just as simplicity is a quality that brings calmness to our outer lives, it is equally a quality to cultivate in our inner world. Meditation is not a path of accumulating theories and information but a path of fos-tering intuition and clarity. Our meditation is not aided by preoccu-pations with goals, evaluation or comparison. Learning to be simply

present, attending wholeheartedly to the moment we are in is the path of meditation. Through habit our minds will demand answers, solutions, reassurance and familiar labels for our experience but this will simply get in the way of clear attentiveness. A major factor in cultivating simplicity is the willingness to let go of all of these demands, to not cling to the variety of thoughts and comparisons that will inevitably arise, but also to let them pass.

Dedication

The central themes of dedication and perseverance run through all great spiritual stories and are essential principles of meditation found in all traditions. As we explore meditation it will not always be a path of exciting revelations and profound breakthroughs. It would be unrealistic to anticipate that every period of meditation will be filled with dazzling insights or states of bliss. Those moments may come to us, but there will also be many moments when it seems that nothing is happening, no progress is being made or when our meditation is felt to be simply boring. There may well also be moments when we are faced with experiences of inner turmoil, states of mind that are challenging or painful inner experiences. This is natural. It is rare for anyone's meditation to unfold in a predictable, linear manner. There will be valleys and peaks, highs and lows, times of delight and times of challenge.

The qualities of dedication and perseverance are essential principles that sustain us on our journey and keep us balanced in the midst of experiences that change in a way that is not always predictable or desired. In moments when we find ourselves despairing over a lack of progress or being assailed by inner storms of thought or feeling it is not time to resign or surrender to despair it is helpful to reflect upon our initial intentions and the vision that began us on our exploration. This should renew our intention to open to and be present with whatever difficulty is before us. Meditation is concerned with awakening, and awakening is an inclusive process – it embraces every aspect of our being and experience, the pleasing and the challenging. Don't judge, don't reject, don't conclude – simply bring a calm, balanced attentiveness to everything that presents itself. The moments when our meditation introduces us to experiences of delight are not times to begin to consider retirement. The capacity to keep coming back and to sustain attention in the midst of highs and lows, the exhilarating and disappointing moments strengthens our inner steadiness and potential for dedication.

Beginning to Meditate

Within the different schools of meditation you will find a range of suggestions about the optimal way to undertake a meditative training. These will range from the traditions that suggest withdrawing from the world into solitude to the traditions that suggest that the most effective way to meditate is in the midst of our daily lives with all their busyness and challenge. Despite these variations it is clear that for meditation to be meaningful and effective for us it must have the capacity to be integrated into the daily rhythms of our lives. Unless we choose a path of withdrawal or asceticism it is realistic to expect that our meditation will have the power to bring not only inner change, but also greater peace and clarity into the whole of our lives. Most of us do not come to meditation looking for a way to separate ourselves from the world even more, but to look for a way to be present in ourselves and in our families, work and play with greater wisdom and compassion.

The majority of meditative traditions will offer a path that embraces the full spectrum of our lives, suggesting the importance of times that are dedicated to a formal cultivation of a practice and the application of this practice on a moment to moment level in every circumstance. The process of transformation is not exclusively concerned with changing our consciousness, but equally with finding the skills to live with well-being, peace and understanding.

Time

Considering the differences in our lifestyles and commitments it is not possible to prescribe what is the right amount of time to dedicate to meditation practice. The rhythm of our lives may allow us to take extended periods of time in more cloistered retreat settings that allow us undertake a dedicated exploration of a meditative discipline. It may also be that the level of our commitments allows only for a regular, daily practice and that our temperament inclines more towards a meditation practice that is developed and integrated on a daily level.

It is helpful to create a time in our day that is regularly dedicated to our formal meditation. When we wake in the morning or before going to bed at night are times that lend themselves well to a period of stillness and reflection. Making these periods of meditation into a reliable part of our daily routine is an invaluable asset in developing a path of practice. We may begin with fifteen-minute or half-hour periods. It is all worthwhile. It is helpful to approach these times with great care – they are not times for rehearsing our day or pondering upon what has been left undone. They are times for focus and dedication.

Place

Just as it is helpful to establish a regular time in our days for formal meditation, it is also helpful to create a space. It is not necessary to retreat to a cave or mountaintop in order to meditate but it is helpful to create a certain simplicity around us that reminds us of the importance of giving care to our inner landscape. It may be simply a corner of our bedroom that becomes a dedicated space. If possible, find a place that is somewhat secluded from excess noise and disturbance. It's time to turn off the telephones and televisions and as much as possible create an external space of silence and calmness.

Posture

Before we ever begin to meditate most of us have been exposed to visual images of what meditation looks like in the form of Buddha statues and other religious images. Some traditions of meditation such as Zen will greatly emphasize the importance of adopting a particular posture whereas other traditions will downplay its significance. Whether you choose to sit in a full lotus position or in a chair there are a few simple guidelines that are helpful.

It is important that you feel at ease and relaxed within your posture. Your meditation will not be overly fruitful if it is spent struggling with excessive discomfort or tension in your body. Meditation is a process of sensitivity and befriending the moment and this begins with the relationship you have with your body. Experiment until you find a posture that you are able to sustain without forcing. It is helpful to sit with an upright back, whether this is on a cushion, on the floor or on a chair. Let your body relax, your eyes can either be closed or simply focused on the floor in front of you. Your body can express the quality of alertness and attentiveness you are seeking in your meditation.

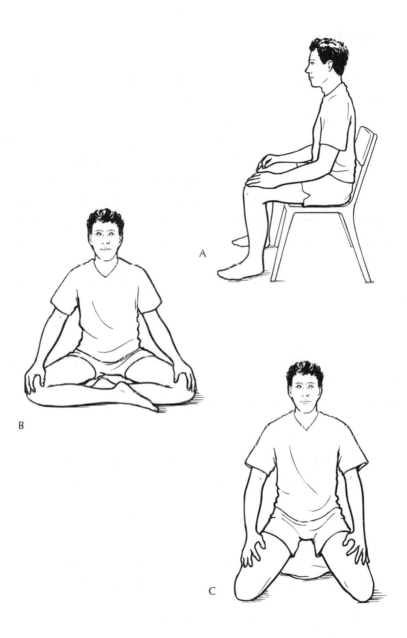

A

B

C

Sitting postures appropriate for meditation

A Teacher

Again, differing degrees of emphasis are given to the significance of having a teacher or guide within the variety of meditative traditions. A teacher will offer more than just instruction in technique or form, but will serve as a spiritual friend able to offer guidance and experience. Some meditators find it helpful to connect with a teacher on an ongoing basis and as our meditation deepens the support of someone who has travelled this path before us can be invaluable. However, a relationship with a teacher is not a prerequisite to cultivating a meditation practice. If you bring to your meditation practice the willingness to learn, to deepen in sensitivity and patience, and the commitment to developing attentiveness, you have everything you need to begin.

In the following chapters the major styles of meditation will be explained. Feel free to experiment with and explore any of them until you find a style you feel some rapport with.

Beginning to Meditate

1 *Choose a regular time – morning, evening, or whenever you can rely upon not being interrupted.*
2 *Find a place – as secluded, simple and quiet as possible.*
3 *Choose a posture that is comfortable for you.*
4 *Set a minimum time for your meditation, whether it is 15, 30 or 45 minutes.*
5 *Check your body for any apparent areas of tension and consciously relax.*
6 *Take a few deep breaths.*
7 *Begin.*

TWO

CONCENTRATION

Within the variety of schools of meditation there is agreement upon the need to cultivate a strong basis of attentiveness or concentration for the development of any style of meditation. Some disciplines will develop concentration as their primary form of practice, whereas other styles will emphasize developing only enough concentration to serve as a foundation for insight, contemplation or devotion. The need to retrain our attention as an essential ingredient in transformation is the central, prevailing thread that runs through the entire variety of meditative disciplines. For depth, balance and understanding a clear and calm attentiveness must first be present.

There are a whole range of experiences that are possible within the field of concentration that run from the simple capacity to keep ourselves focused in the present moment upon a single subject without distractedness, to profound altered states of consciousness that bring with them experiences of bliss, oneness and absorption in which the activities of the body and mind are stilled. Visionary experiences and feelings of deep rapture, joy and equanimity are all experiences that emerge from deep levels of concentration. Within this whole spectrum of experience the essential benefits of concentration to steady and calm the mind and establish us in the present moment are recognized.

Through developing concentration the mind is brought to rest in the present moment and deepening levels of calm pervade both mind and body. Through focusing our attention upon a single object there is an integration of the mind, body and present moment, and our capacity to attend to one moment at a time with clarity and sensitivity is enhanced. We are enabled to attend to the inner landscape of sensations, thoughts and feelings that is revealed to us free of our usual habitual reactions of judging or resistance. The concentrated mind has the power to penetrate deeply into the processes of our minds and bodies and to explore with ease other dimensions of meditation. Concentration enables us to cut through the habits of restlessness, discursive thinking and reactions that entangle us and set our minds in motion; the mind becomes tranquil and serene.

Through both fairly shallow and very profound states of concentration there are a number of insights that can emerge that bring deeper levels of happiness, harmony and freedom into our lives. In the calm and serenity that develop through concentration practice we discover subtle yet pronounced levels of happiness that are qualitatively different than the fleeting states of happiness or pleasure we find through excitement, achievement or possession. It is an inner happiness and contentment that depends on nothing outside of ourselves bringing with it a greater sense of inner completeness. This understanding changes our relationship to the world around us, enabling us to let go with greater ease and step back from the relentless pursuit of consumption, attainment and possession. Resting within an inner serenity and richness we are less inclined to search the world for the happiness we feel to be missing inwardly. We learn to be at ease within ourselves and within each moment – we find ourselves in greater harmony with the world around us and with other people. Through the development of concentration the mind becomes less fragile and susceptible to extremes. It becomes steady and balanced – able to receive the variety of experiences and impressions that come to us in life without feeling overwhelmed or burdened.

Concentration practice greatly enhances inner confidence as we improve in the art of attending wholeheartedly to one moment at a time. We develop our inner resources of energy, attentiveness and dedication and through collecting and directing them towards the present moment or a single subject of meditation we discover the calmness and clarity born of our own efforts. In becoming increasingly familiar with deeper levels of calmness the mind loses its addiction to busyness and entanglement. There is a lessening of interest in fantasy and daydreams that offer limited satisfaction in the light of a calm and clear attentiveness. Anxiety and stress levels decrease as they are supplanted by deepening levels of well-being and serenity. The inner tranquillity that emerges enables us to respond more intuitively and clearly both to our inner and outer world rather than being compelled by habitual reaction. The nature of the mind changes through concentration practice and our sense of the possibilities that lie within our consciousness expands.

Concentration is a means of simplifying our inner landscape. Rather than experiencing ourselves as being a captive of the endless stream of random thoughts, memories, plans and images that pass through our minds, concentration frees us from entanglement. As our attention deepens the thoughts begin to slow down and become clearer to us. We find an increasing capacity to be able to let go of the mind's dominance and a deeper quality of calmness and clarity begins to emerge. We are aware of thinking, aware of the beginnings and endings of thoughts with a calm and clear attentiveness. Agitation is replaced by calmness, habit replaced by sensitivity and confusion gives way to clarity.

Concentration is developed through focusing the mind upon a single subject. Through this attentiveness the mind is united with the present moment. The subject that is chosen for attention will differ according to the meditation style, it can be a visual object, a sound or the breath, but the objective of sustaining a focus remains the same. The intention is to cultivate an undistracted and undivided attentiveness. The subject that is chosen serves as a steady anchor, a lifeline amidst the swirls of thoughts, images and sensation. It is a place we continually and gently return to each time we become lost or entangled in the streams of activity that pass through our minds. The sustaining of the focus upon a single object requires both perseverance and patience as we are faced again and again with the habitual wandering of the mind as it departs into past and future. We are facing the habit of distractedness that has perhaps accompanied us through our lives. It is not willpower or striving that enables us to penetrate this habit but practice, consistency and the right spirit of dedication and acceptance. Meditation is an art and like the exploration of any other discipline it requires love, the willingness to learn and the capacity to accept the moments we falter.

The nature of the mind is to have thoughts, images, plans and memories. Concentration practice is not an endeavour to suppress any of this; it is only in very profound states of concentration that the mind will actually come to total stillness. Any attempt to resist or push away the thoughts that arise will only increase their intensity. A gentle but consistent returning of the attention to the selected focus is the way to bring the mind to calmness. Meditation is not anti-thought nor is it in the service of dismissing the value and capacities of our mind. The mind has a remarkable potential for creativity, reflection, clarity and investigation. Concentration enhances our ability to use and apply thought creatively and appropriately, rather than be dominated or overwhelmed by excess thinking.

The way of developing concentration is to plant in the foreground of our attention a single subject which we consistently focus upon and return to rather than becoming entangled in any of the stream of events that are occurring in our mind and body. By sustaining this focus the mind will naturally and gradually slow down and the swirl of thoughts will to differing degrees begin to calm and take their place in the background of our consciousness rather than ensnaring us. As our capacity for attention develops it will be increasingly natural for our minds to rest in the focus of our meditation and differing degrees of unity will begin to emerge. There is a growing happiness and sense of wellbeing as we pass though the variety of resistances such as restlessness or dullness that present themselves and the mind finds a certain steadiness and ease in its attention.

Almost anything will serve as a focus for concentration, different temperaments will find affinity with different subjects as the focus for their attention. It is certainly helpful to choose as an object for focus something relatively simple and familiar to us. If we initially select an intricate mandala or complex series of phrases we will make the task of cultivating attention unnecessarily difficult. As our skill in concentration develops we may well choose to direct it towards increasingly complex subjects but in the beginning simplicity is most conducive to calmness.

Exploring the Path of Concentration

Finding a suitable place to practise, adopting a posture that is comfortable to us and bringing to our meditation the spirit of patience and acceptance, we can begin to explore some of the paths of concentration that are widely taught. Don't be tempted to rush or be overly ambitious, every moment of cultivating attention and oneness is worthwhile. The fruits of our meditation may not be immediately visible to us in the form of tangible results or grand experiences and breakthroughs. Yet every moment we are engaged in bringing our attention back to clarity and single pointedness we are directly engaged in the transformation of our being. We are following the pathways of patience, dedication, clarity and compassion rather than the familiar pathways of resistance, distractedness and reaction.

Initially as you practise you will find that your attention repeatedly wanders away from your chosen subject, becoming lost in memories of the past, plans for the future or preoccupations in the present. We may no sooner return our attention to the present than it departs once more remembering a conversation we had yesterday. We may be tempted to try and analyze the thoughts that present themselves, wonder at their hidden meaning or try to evaluate our progress. It is not uncommon to feel that meditation has produced even more thoughts than before we began to practise. It is more likely we are simply becoming aware of the relentless nature of thought, produced by the mind untrained in attentiveness. Distractedness is a habit of the mind – we are gently learning to disentangle, training the mind in simplicity and clarity. The moment you notice that your attention has wandered away is a moment of returning to attentiveness. Don't judge or become frustrated with your wandering, simply anchor your attention once more in your meditation subject and begin again. Learning to be attentive you need the patience of a child learning to walk.

Concentration with Visual Subjects

A candle flame, a shape, a symbolic object, a mandala or a colour can all serve equally well as a focus for developing attention. The concentration cultivated in relationship to these subjects may serve as a foundation for other devotional and visualization practices later on in the path but initially the objective is to develop a sustained and steady attentiveness. We are integrating our mind and body with the subject of our meditation through sustained attention.

An example of a mandala

Settle yourself in a relaxed and alert posture then place your chosen visual meditation subject just in front of you and bring your eyes to rest upon it. Gently settle your gaze and allow your mind and body to relax. Don't let your eyes wander around the room but simply fasten your attention upon the object in front of you. Whatever thoughts or bodily sensations arise, give them minimal attention – simply let them flow through you and pass away. As you begin to feel connected with your visual subject, let your eyes close and sustain the visual impression of your subject in your mind. In the beginning you may only be able to do this for a few moments before the visual impression becomes vague or lost. When this happens open your eyes once more and bring your gaze to rest again upon the object in front of you. You may need to do this many times before you find you are able to retain the visual impression of your subject within your mind for longer periods.

As the concentration deepens you will find it less necessary to revert to the external visual connection with your subject as its image becomes more clearly imprinted upon your consciousness in an increasingly sustained way. The image will become increasingly clear in detail and vividness and there will be a greater ease in holding it in the forefront of your consciousness. The thoughts or images that previously appeared to clamour for your attention will begin to quiet and become like whispers arising and passing in the background of your consciousness. This is a sign that your concentration is deepening. Whenever you become distracted, know that you can always open your eyes and return to the direct visual connection with your subject.

As your concentration begins to deepen you may discover that you only need to make a very brief contact with the external visual image in order to trigger the inner imprint. The capacity to recall that inner visual image brings with it qualities of calmness and well-being in the mind and body. In deeper levels of concentration the distance or separation between the image and the observer begins to disappear and there is the sense of being absorbed within the visual impression. This experience of absorption triggers deeper levels of happiness, joy and communion. There are different levels of absorption it is possible to realize. The body and mind can become profoundly still to the point where they make no impression upon the consciousness and there is a sense of being saturated with a sublime peace and bliss. It takes considerable practice to reach states of deeper absorption – you should not feel disillusioned if in the early stages of your practice you seem to spend more time disentangling your attention from thought than floating in bliss.

WAY of

Concentration with Sounds

Within every spiritual tradition the use of sound plays a central role in cultivating both concentration and devotion, whether we chant the name of God or use the repetition of classical phrases or prayers to collect our attention. Again a vast variety of sounds can serve as an object of concentration upon which to focus our attention. Mantras, prayers, phrases, chants and the repetition of symbolic religious words are all sounds that are adopted as a basis for collecting our attention. Some styles of meditation will encourage the verbal repetition of the sounds, others will promote a silent rendering of the sound. There are schools of meditation that encourage the continued repetition of the sound throughout all of our daily life activities and others that encourage its cultivation only in times of formal meditation.

The objective is the same in both schools of emphasis – the attention is turned inwardly and focused wholeheartedly upon the sound. The intention is to cultivate a direct connection and eventually an absorption into the sound. Once more the repetition and resultant concentration serve as a foundation for further devotional or contemplative practices where there is equally an absorption into the spiritual qualities represented by the sound, phrase or prayer.

In choosing a sound to serve as a central anchor for your concentration the principles of simplicity and familiarity again hold some significance. Whether we choose the sound of OM or a simple prayer or inspirational quote, the practice begins with the slow and consistent repetition of it. Some people choose simple statements such as, 'May I be filled with compassion', or 'May all beings live in peace' as a focus that is both evocative and symbolic. A single word such as 'peace' or 'calm' will serve. Through our sustained focus it becomes more prominent to us than any of the other mental or physical events that are occurring. It is important that the repetition doesn't become mechanical or habitual but through giving each utterance of the sound our wholehearted attentiveness, it is an expression of sensitivity and meaning. Through repeating the sound we become increasingly attuned and close to it. Again many times our attention will depart to become entangled elsewhere, the cultivation of concentration occurs through the same gentle returning of attention to our primary object of focus. As we continue with the practice, our attunement with the sound deepens and it becomes an integral part of our consciousness, easily accessible to us. In the deepening of the practice the level of attunement with the sound becomes so profound that it saturates our being and we are absorbed in it. The characteristics of absorption are always joy and oneness. Even on more surface levels of connection with our chosen sound it offers us a refuge of calm and focus that we are then able to bring to the variety of circumstances in our lives where there is turmoil or confusion. The chosen sound, mantra or phrase provides a tangible place to anchor our attention in times of stress or even in the midst of activities that require little attention.

Concentration on Breathing

The practice of focusing upon our own breathing process as a means of cultivating one-pointedness and concentration is found within a variety of schools of meditation practice. This widely cultivated practice is adopted for a number of reasons: it is a style of practice that is unencumbered by religious connotations and therefore has a universal appeal, the focusing upon our breathing process does not demand that we concentrate on anything culturally unknown or unfamiliar to us, the breath is immediately accessible to us. No matter what else is happening in our lives, no matter what circumstances we find ourselves in – we are always breathing. Our breath is always available to us as an anchor of attentiveness.

It is a practice blessed with great simplicity. As in any other form of concentration practice the objective is to cultivate a clearly focused, undistracted attentiveness, to calm and clear the mind, to establish us in the present moment and to bring serenity and joy. Like any other form of concentration practice, the practice of attending to our breath can be developed into deep states of absorption with experiences of sublime joy and equanimity, or developed just sufficiently enough to serve as a foundation for exploring other dimensions of meditation and the development of understanding. There are a number of schools of meditation that suggest developing the principle of clearly established attentiveness utilizing the breath, prior to expanding the focus of meditation to develop insight.

There are a variety of ways of cultivating concentration through attending to our breathing process. No one of them is intrinsically superior or more effective than another – again different temperaments will find a greater sense of harmony in slightly different variations upon what is essentially a single path of establishing and developing attentiveness.

Counting

After settling your body in your chosen meditation posture turn your attention inwardly to be aware of your breathing process. Don't attempt to alter or control your breathing – it will not accelerate your capacity to concentrate – but simply attend to the natural rhythm of your breath. The purpose of counting is to aid us in focusing our attention upon our breath and bring us closer to each breath as it occurs. As you breathe in, silently count one, as you breathe out count two. Continue up until ten and then begin again with one. There will be times when your attention becomes lost in a thought process – the moment you become aware of this simply return to counting one and continue. Continue with the counting until your attention begins to feel steady and established in your breathing process and then let the counting go, remembering that the counting is only a tool to establish your attention.

Fixing the Attention

As you begin your meditation, initially bring your attention to the whole movement of your breath from its beginning to end and notice the way in which your body responds to each inhalation and each exhalation – the movements of expansion and contraction. Notice in which part of your body you most clearly perceive your breath – it may be in the area of your upper lip and the entrance to your nostrils, the area of your chest or in the rise and fall of your abdomen. Establish your attention in the area of your body where your breath is most clearly perceptible and cultivate a sustained and unwavering focus at your upper lip, chest or abdomen. Notice the sensations that arise in this area of your body as you breathe in and out, whether coolness, warmth, rising or falling – not evaluating them but bringing a mindful attentiveness. Again your attention will be at times pulled away by thoughts, sounds or sensations, the moment you are aware this has taken place simply return your attention once more to the area of your body you have selected. As the mind calms and steadies you will notice changes both in the state of your body and in the rhythm of your breathing. Your body will begin to relax and feel lighter, your breathing will become more subtle and slow. Don't interfere in any way with this natural unfoldment, but keep the attention unwavering upon your chosen focus.

Naming

As you begin your meditation and turn your attention to your breathing process, naming is another means of connecting your attention more closely with your breath. As you breathe, silently make a mental note of in-breath, as you breathe out silently make a mental note of out-breath. The words rising, falling, expansion or contraction can be gently attached to each movement. Continue to note each inhalation and each exhalation as they occur. The purpose of using these labels is to bring the attention closer to the actual experience of each breath as it occurs. Care needs to be taken in using the mental notes so they neither become habitual nor inter-fere with the direct perception of the breath on a moment to moment level. The introduction of naming is an effective way of bringing the mind to calmness and one-pointedness, particularly in times when it is particularly agitated or busy. As the mind calms and the attention begins to stabilize the mental notes will fade in significance and drop away.

Bare Attention

After settling yourself in your posture and turning your attention to your breath, again sense in your body the entire movement of your breath from beginning to end. Notice the slight pause between the ending of one out breath and the beginning of the next in breath. Let your attention move in harmony with the movement of each breath, following its progress from your nostrils to your abdomen and the movements of your body as the breath is released. Notice the sensation of your breath as it enters your body and passes through your throat, the expansion and contraction of your chest and the rise and fall of your abdomen. When distracted, again simply return your attention to the next breath to begin again.

Concentration with Phrases

Some schools of meditation will elect to bond particular phrases with each breath as it occurs. The purpose of this bonding is to remind us of the deeper objectives of our practice which is not to become a perfect breather nor just to achieve altered states of experience, but to awaken us and to cultivate the qualities of heart and mind that enable us to live with greater wisdom and compassion. The phrases can vary enormously; some of the frequently used phrases are ones that express particular qualities of heart and mind. As you breathe in you may silently repeat 'breathing in calmness', or 'breathing in peace' and silently repeat the utterance in harmony with the out breath. You may choose to harmonize the phrase 'May I be filled with peace', or 'May I be free from fear' with each breath.

Again there are some fundamental guidelines to be aware of as you use phrases with your breathing. Keep them simple, too many words will make your meditation too conceptual. Use phrases that genuinely express your inner aspirations in meditation, the qualities you are seeking to cultivate or embody. Link your phrase with each breath closely, so they do not become habitual and can be founded upon a true sense of meaningfulness.

Moment to Moment Concentration

This practice is focused upon developing a powerful and steady attentiveness which, instead of selecting a subject of meditation that excludes every other phenomenon that arises in the moment, is inclusive. It is a practice of cultivating a wholehearted attentiveness that is directed towards whatever aspect of our experience is most predominant in any moment. It is a fluid attentiveness that can shift between the breath, body sensations, sounds, thoughts, feelings and sights – giving to each moment an attention that is directly and clearly perceiving whatever is taking place.

In this style of moment to moment concentration, the breath is frequently adopted as being the central anchor of concentration where the attention rests and the focus it returns to when distracted or unsteady. When the attention is drawn away from the breath to another area of our experience that has become more predominant, such as sensations, sounds or thoughts, it is intentionally directed to that area to know clearly with bare attention whatever is being experienced. Whether the object that the attention is directed towards is a sound or a body sensation is secondary in importance; primary is the cultivation of one-pointedness, clear seeing and calmness.

Sometimes mental noting is attached to this development of bare attention. When the attention is drawn to a sound, the mental note of hearing is brought in; when drawn to a thought the mental note that most appropriately describes the theme of that thought is brought, such as memory, planning, fantasy, etc. When the attention is drawn to a sensation in your body, the mental note of feeling, pain, warmth, etc, is brought. The mental notes need to be used in the spirit of simplicity; they are not a means to evaluate or analyze what is taking place but simply an aid to seeing the movements of the mind more clearly. The various movements and changes within the mind–body process are held in the light of a clear and simple attention – the attention is then returned to the primary anchor point of the breath.

This is a style of concentration meditation which can be cultivated equally in both formal meditation periods and in the midst of our daily activities such as walking, doing the laundry, taking a shower. The attention is increasingly attuned to the present moment and whatever is taking place within in. Nothing is considered to be a distraction; but whatever is occurring in any moment is seen as an invitation to develop a mind of steadiness and clear seeing. It is a path of attentiveness that makes a tangible difference in the quality of our actions and movements as we cultivate wholeheartedness and sensitivity. Every moment of our life becomes an integral part of our meditative path.

Obstacles in Concentration Practice

Concentration practice is simple but not easy and inevitably there are a number of obstacles we will meet in our journey that have a universal quality to them. The obstacles and challenges that we encounter in our meditation practice are the same forces of heart and mind that can create confusion in the rest of our lives. Dullness, restlessness, negativity, desire and doubt are not states that exclusively arise in those moments we sit down to meditate. They are habitual and powerful patterns that can equally arise in many moments of our lives. Our meditation practice provides the opportunity to learn to skilfully address these states; a skill that can be integrated into the whole of our lives.

Already mentioned is the habit of distractedness, wandering and being lost in random thinking that can lead to so much fragmentation and disconnection in our lives. This inclination of mind is not ended through judgement, will-power or resistance but is calmed and focused through patience and perseverance. At some point in their practice most people will encounter the hindrance or mental state of dullness or sleepiness. We attempt to focus our attention yet feel that we are sinking in heaviness, weariness or boredom and our attention becomes dissipated. Dullness is not a disaster, at times it is born of genuine tiredness or stress, other times it is a form of resistance that arises. When it is present, meditate for a time with your eyes open, check that your body is alert and upright, ensure your meditation space is not overly warm or stuffy or simply do your meditation practice standing up. When the mind feels heavy or sluggish it is helpful to use counting or naming to stay in touch with the breathing process.

Restlessness comes in a number of different forms – sometimes the mind becomes very agitated and full, sometimes it feels impossible to keep the body still, other times the quality of attention is unsettled and superficial. In times of restlessness, ensure that you bring to your posture an intentional relaxation and stillness. Notice where there is tension in your body and consciously relax. When restless it is helpful to be more precise in your concentration – counting or naming become valuable assets in these moments.

Few people in meditation practice will not undergo periods of doubt – times when we question the worth of what we are undertaking, times when we doubt our progress or feel that we are ultimately incapable of developing any depth in our meditation. Again this experience is natural and somewhat inevitable. Meditation is not linear in its development, nor will anyone's meditation be a path of undiluted bliss and breakthrough. The experience of doubt produces many thoughts, often flavoured by judgement or anxiety. There are times in our lives when thought is creative and supportive, in times of doubt our thoughts are rarely our friend. When rooted in doubt our thoughts tend to assume forms that undermine our confidence, effort and dedication. It is helpful to remind ourselves in periods of doubt of the aspirations and intentions we began our practice with and to be able to see this experience as a phase we are passing through rather than any form of believable conclusion.

The hindrance of wanting will also arrive – we want our experience to be different than it is, to have different thoughts, experiences and feelings than the ones that are present. We are aware of our ambitions, demands and expectations and the mind becomes filled with thoughts of what 'should' be happening. Our expectations lead us to want to reject the moment we are in and jump into a better, more ideal moment. As we become increasingly critical of our present experience the tendency to fantasize becomes more pronounced. In these moments we need to remind ourselves that this is where we learn some of the primary transforming qualities of meditation – acceptance, harmony with what is and understanding.

The reverse side of this force of wanting is aversion, dislike or resistance. Anger, judgement, prejudice and negativity are all forms of aversion that will reveal themselves to us as we practice. They are not signals of spiritual failure but part of the process of becoming more aware of our inner landscape. Just as they are feelings that arise in our lives they will also appear in our meditation. We should investigate them briefly as we experience them – where do we sense anger in our bodies, how does it feel, what form of thoughts does it produce. It is a time for gentleness and kindness in our attention. Do not try to erase or avoid the aversions that arise, but include them in the light of your attention.

Obstacles do arise in our meditation, they need to be accepted as part of our path and our practice. With attention they can be observed, penetrated and understood. With the right spirit they are not enemies to be overcome but doors to new ways of being and understanding that are rooted in wisdom and compassion. Our meditation does not begin in the moment when we have succeeded in banishing all obstacles and difficulties from our consciousness or life. It is in these moments of challenge that our meditation becomes truly relevant – a pathway to peace and understanding.

The benefits of concentration practice are varied and profound. It will bring increasing depths of inner calmness and stillness to our inner and outer lives. In deeper states of development concentration can lead to enriching altered states of consciousness that feature profound joy, oneness and unshakeable balance – experiences which in themselves can lead to a deepening in faith, dedication and understanding. The development of calm and clear attentiveness will enable us to think more clearly and creatively, give us more immediate access to intuitive ways of seeing and will calm our bodies and minds. It is a practice that will touch and affect all of our lives giving us the ability to focus more clearly and calmly upon the myriad of tasks and challenges we encounter and respond to them with wholeheartedness and one-pointedness. Concentration practice deepens inner confidence and provides a foundation for exploring other dimensions of meditation with greater ease and immediacy. Our capacity for appreciation, sensitivity and responsiveness is profoundly enhanced.

Possible Concentration Subjects

1   *A visual subject – a flower, a candle flame, a symbolic object or shape.*
2   *Sounds – a single word or phrase, chant or prayer.*
3   *The breath – counting, naming or bare attention.*

THREE

MINDFULNESS
Meditation

Within every great meditative tradition from Buddhism to Sufism there will be found elements of mindfulness. The heart of mindfulness meditation is the development of wisdom – a deepening understanding of ourselves and life. All spiritual teaching will agree that it is profound understanding that liberates us from the constraints of habit, conditioning and limitation. Through cultivating a moment-to-moment attentiveness there begins to emerge a clear and penetrating awareness vaster than our conceptual mind. Beneath the variety of differences that are present amongst the myriad spiritual disciplines, awareness is the key to transformation. For anything at all to change in our lives, we must first be aware – clearly immediately connected to the present moment.

Some spiritual disciplines will emphasize mindfulness as being the umbrella under which all specific techniques of meditation will be developed. In other traditions mindfulness is a finely formulated practice taught in a number of different styles. One of the great gifts of mindfulness meditation is that it can be developed and practised in any posture, in any circumstance – it is learning to shine the light of clear, mindful attentiveness upon every moment of our experience. It is a practice that is primarily dedicated to awakening us to what is true and actual in all of our perceptions and our responses to them. Through this clear and immediate perception insight, or wisdom, emerges, transforming us and our lives.

Mindfulness is qualitatively different from concentration practice. Where concentration practice is exclusive, focusing upon a single object while excluding other aspects of our experience, mindfulness meditation is inclusive. Our bodies, minds, feelings, mental states, perceptions, sounds and sight are all equally embraced in the clear, sensitive light of mindfulness without preference or distinction. Whatever is happening in any moment invites the application of mindfulness. Mindfulness meditation cultivates a quality of whole-hearted listening – a listening to our changing inner experience and an equal listening to the changing landscape of each moment, without judgement or preference.

Exploration and investigation is an equally significant principle of mindfulness meditation. Our listening to our inner and outer worlds is not just superficial or conceptual but carries with it the intention to understand what is actually taking place beneath our concepts, thoughts or ideas of what is occurring. Mindfulness is concerned not with just thinking about the present moment but with direct experience. This capacity to penetrate deeply, to see clearly and to be wholeheartedly present in one moment at a time is the beginning of understanding.

Mindfulness meditation does hold within it an element of concentration that provides a strong and steady foundation for the development of insight. It is the quality of concentration of bare attention that is brought to each moment of our changing experience – to be fully present in that moment without distractedness or wavering. In mindfulness meditation the focus of attention will shift in accord with the moment-to-moment changes that occur in our experience. The breath may still serve as our primary anchor of attentiveness, yet an equality of attentiveness is brought to sights, sounds, thoughts, feelings and sensations as they emerge. The foundation of steadiness and clarity provided through concentration and bare attention is the factor that allows understanding to penetrate deeply and to transform. Concentration provides the power through which insight can deepen.

In our journey of meditation there are many new and liberating insights that will be revealed to us. It is also true that we begin on the path of meditation with a variety of insights that have been garnered throughout our lives. Through our own life experience we frequently know well the pathways we can follow that lead to confusion and conflict and the pathways we can follow that lead to harmony and happiness. We know well the consequences of being entangled in anger, greed or fear just as we know the effects of being deeply connected with qualities of forgiveness, generosity and happiness. We know the quality of our life suffers through being entangled in preoccupations with the past or future and we know how our life is enriched through feeling a direct and sensitive connection with the present. We know what it feels like to be lost in confusion and we often know the ways in which that confusion is generated through misunderstanding or seeing through the filters of fear, anger or anxiety.

We also frequently encounter the frustration of feeling a separation or gap between our intellectual knowledge concerning confusion and its cause and our capacity to integrate that knowledge into our lives in a way that ends such confusion. It is not an absence of insight that is the source of our frustration but the reality that the insight and understanding already present in us does not penetrate deeply enough to bring about real transformation. One of the benefits of establishing a clear, steady foundation of bare attention is that it dissolves the gap that can exist between knowing something and actually living in accord with and embodying our own understanding. The mind that is settled with ease and calmness in the present moment is deeply receptive to insight and a cellular level of transformation. The mind that is entangled in a swirl of thoughts and images catches glimpses of insight but they tend to be more superficial and random, without the capacity to transform. As our attentiveness slows down the stream of inner busyness every moment is highlighted in the light of sensitivity and clarity of vision.

The purpose of insight, developed through mindfulness meditation, is to awaken and liberate us from the entanglements of our beliefs, images, prejudices and habits which blind us to seeing things as they truly are. Mindfulness brings us close to each moment, calmly and alertly present in a way that dissolves the power of our habitual reactions and beliefs. Mindfulness is the capacity to see things deeply, beneath the level of concepts and opinions – seeing what is actual and true enables us to let go of all that is false and distorting.

The practice of mindfulness meditation is presented in a variety of different ways. Beneath the superficial differences of the different techniques and forms of this meditation, the core element of deepening in understanding and awakening as a path to deep transformation and liberation prevails. Mindfulness, developed through meditation practice, is also more than just a technique cultivated in formal meditation. Increasingly as it is applied it touches all of our lives, whether we are in formal meditation or not. We find ourselves more deeply wakeful, able to see clearly and committed to discovering what is true and actual. Awareness becomes the natural resting place of our minds; it has the characteristic of illuminating each moment and intrinsically carries within it the qualities of sensitivity, openness, alertness and balance.

There are several essential principles of mindfulness meditation that will be found in all of the varying styles it is practised in.

Sensitivity

One of these principles is that mindfulness practice is a moment-to-moment application of sensitivity. Whatever presents itself to our attention in any moment, from our inner or outer world is deemed to be worthy of our wholehearted attention. There is nothing that is judged to be unworthy, irrelevant or mundane. In mindfulness meditation sounds, sights, thoughts or body sensations are all greeted equally in the light of mindful attention. All are welcomed and seen as an invitation to be fully present, to see clearly and deserving of sensitivity. This equality of attentiveness means a withdrawal of our judgements of good and bad, significant or insignificant, better and worse. There is a dropping away of our ideas of what 'should' be happening or how something 'should' be. There is just what is, as it is – free from our prejudices and associations. In mindfulness meditation we are not invited to draw endless conclusions about what we are attending to in the present moment, not to compare or evaluate, but simply to be there fully. As we bring this clear, sensitive attentiveness to every moment we notice the changes in how we relate and respond to our changing experience and perceptions. Mindfulness brings us closer to the moment – we see, listen, touch and feel more deeply and simply. A profound quality of sensitivity begins to emerge as we learn to listen well and be fully present. We begin to have a glimpse of what it means to see anew in each moment. There is a vitality and freshness in all of our perceptions. We are increasingly able to enter into each moment like a visitor – open, sensitive and willing to learn.

Oneness

Equally an aspect of this sensitivity is that we begin to contact a deeper level of communion and oneness within all of the activities of our lives. Mindfulness has a powerful integrating element, bonding body, heart, mind and present moment. When we walk we just walk without endlessly entertaining all of our thoughts about our destination. When we wash the dishes we approach that task with the same spirit of mindfulness as we approach our formal meditation. When we listen to another person speak, we attend fully instead of being lost in all of our stories and conclusions about them. We become increasingly appreciative and wholehearted in our lives – connected with the vitality and richness of each moment.

One of the key ingredients of mindfulness is that it is receptive rather than reactive, more concerned with the quality of our presence in each moment than with the results we produce. The experience of oneness that evolves through mindfulness means that there is a significant dropping away of habit in our lives – a falling away of the habits within our actions and speech and a falling away of our habitual reactions of mind and heart. Habit divorces us from the richness of each moment and numbs us, making us mechanical in our actions and responses. Mindfulness awakens and sensitizes us as we are established in the present moment.

Clarity

The mindfulness that is brought to each moment is not a vague, wandering quality of attention that just skims over each momentary thought or perception. It is clear and steady, attending to whatever is predominant in the moment – one sound at a time, one sensation at a time, one thought at a time. Mindfulness is like a mirror, simply reflecting without preference what is actually occurring in each moment. It is not concerned with where a thought or sound or sensation came from or where it disappears to, but is simply attuned to the changing nature of our experience. Liking or disliking, pleasant or unpleasant sensations, feelings or thoughts are not experiences that trigger the application or withdrawal of mindfulness but attract the same clear attentiveness. In the light of this unwavering, clear mindfulness it is as if each moment is revealed to us fully. Our habit of surrounding the perceptions of each moment with judgement and reaction has a long history – mindfulness dissolves the habit enabling us to perceive with both simplicity and calmness.

Present Moment

Mindfulness meditation is not concerned with attempting to ana-lyze our past with all of its memories and experiences that are so frequently superimposed upon the present. Neither is it concerned with attempting to safeguard or plan the future. It is a present moment practice in which thoughts of both past and future will arise and pass in the light of mindfulness. The understandings that allow us to be at peace with the past and enter into the next moment, the future, with confidence and ease emerge from the mindfulness, clarity and calmness we find in the present moment. Mindfulness is like a bridge of connectedness, establishing us in the moment that is occurring with sensitivity and alertness – this is the only moment we can transform.

Investigation

Mindfulness meditation has an investigative quality within it that fosters our intuitive potential – the capacity to see the essence of each moment and everything that occurs within it, free of the distorting factors of projection, holding or resistance. That quality of investigation is directed toward understanding not only what is happening to us in each moment – the sounds, sights, thoughts and events we encounter, but equally to clearly perceive what is hap-pening within us in relationship to these changing impressions and events. Through mindfulness we strip away the colouring of judgement, concept, fantasy and fear with which we often habitually surround these events and learn to see them as they actually are.

The same mindfulness is brought to explore the variety of responses that arise within us as the events and impressions within our experience change. We become increasingly aware of the movement of fear, anger, projection, expectation and the whole range of emotions and thoughts with which we colour and distort the impressions and events in our lives. Liking, disliking, rejecting, pursuing, being for or against are the familiar pathways of the mind when it is not established in clear attentiveness. Mindfulness enables us to step back to the point of receiving our inner and outer world, before the processes of conceptualizing and reacting begin. It is a place of pure awareness that is not inclined to add or subtract anything at all to what is being experienced. It is equally a place of profound balance, clarity and responsiveness.

Cultivating these skills we are free to explore and understand the most complex of our inner processes and emotions. The depressions, anxieties, obsessions and fears we so habitually flee from because they threaten to overwhelm us can be explored, accepted and understood. Mindfulness condemns nothing but brings a non-judgemental observation. It allows us to understand those aspects of ourselves we may have previously rejected and denied. Nor does mindfulness make any attempt to modify what we might label as being negative into something more positive. It simply sees what is there. In mindfulness we do not become infatuated with the range of experiences we call pleasant or flattering. These too are embraced with an equality of attentiveness. There is a natural dropping away of confusion and the emergence of clarity and balance.

Intention

The intention to be present and to understand all things as they actually are, free from any distortion, is an essential ingredient in deepening mindfulness and insight. Mindfulness practice seeks to foster a deeper understanding of peace, compassion, the nature of ourselves and all life and the capacity to live in accord with those insights. It is the intention to see clearly, to awaken and transform that distinguishes the mindfulness of the meditator from the kind of attention a burglar may bring to a break-in or a tightrope walker to crossing a bar. Clear intention cultivates exploration, investigation and understanding. It frees us to explore our most complex emotions and inner processes and begin to understand them intuitively.

Seeing What is True

Mindfulness meditation not only cultivates a clear perception of what is actually happening around us and within us, but also fosters a clear understanding of the true nature of all of those experiences. We begin to see the processes involved in the formulation of our thoughts, emotions and reactions. The changing nature of all of those processes is perceived more immediately. The previously perceived solidity of our inner experiences becomes more transparent to us. We learn to dive beneath our concepts and conclusions about each moment and directly see what is occurring. This is the wisdom element of mindfulness meditation that awakens and liberates. Mindfulness meditation does not attempt to impose some new belief system or theory upon our inner and outer universe but lets us see what is essentially true in our changing world of experience and what is false or untrue.

Applications of Mindfulness

There are essentially three areas to which mindfulness is directed with the intention to bring clarity and understanding. The first of these areas is the dimension of our lives we could refer to as our personal story, the dynamics of our inner world.

Personal Story

Mindfulness is a journey of self-discovery – learning to be intimate with ourselves. It is not a journey of narcissism – there is no intention to modify our personalities, to perfect ourselves or achieve any particular elevated image of holiness. It is not a path of self improvement. There is much that will undergo change in our inner world through the application of mindfulness but the intention is always one of seeing clearly and fostering understanding. Through mindfulness we explore our inner landscape; the world of our bodies, feelings, mental states and contents of our mind. As we initiate this exploration with calmness and clarity of seeing, free from all judgements and conclusions, we begin to perceive with balance and sensitivity the variety of changes our inner world goes through in every moment. We wake up to our inner life. Rather than living with the retrospective knowledge well known to us in our lives, where we look back on the past with regret or remorse, wondering how we could have responded differently, our seeing becomes immediate, direct and deep.

Mindfulness of Body

We explore the life of our bodies with greater sensitivity, seeing directly the body-mind relationship. Mindfulness is a willingness to open to and see fully the variety of physical experiences our bodies go through. There are experiences of pleasure and experiences of pain within our bodies, just as there are in all of life. Exploring our relationship to this spectrum of pain and pleasure within our bodies becomes a microcosmic view of how we relate to pain and pleasure in every area of our lives. Habitually we flee from the unpleasant and pursue the pleasant. Accustomed to fleeing from the painful in our inner or outer lives, we learn to fear it, avoid it, suppress it and so live a life of struggle and anxiety. With mindfulness we bring a balanced and calm attention to explore and stay present with the whole spectrum of physical experience as it is happening. We learn to befriend our bodies and our whole relationship to our physical life can be transformed. Giving attention to our bodies in a variety of postures whether sitting, standing or walking, to the rhythms of our breathing, to the different layers of sensation that emerge in our bodies we learn to bring balance and clarity to our relationship with all sensations. With a calm body, there is a releasing not only of superficial tensions, but often also of deeply buried areas of pain created through emotional or psychological trauma. Mindfulness brings an integration of body and mind.

Mindfulness of our Inner World

Mindfulness allows us to see with clarity and balance the movements of our minds and feelings. We see the forces of anger, fear, greed or confusion in which we can become lost and the way in which these forces lead to pain and struggle in our lives. We see the ways in which we can colour and distort our inner and outer world through projection, judgement and the associations from the past. We see the ways in which our moment-to-moment experience of life is shaped and moulded by the quality of our relationship to it. Exploring our inner world is not only bad news, we also see the forces of compassion, generosity, sensitivity and love that move within us and lead to happiness and harmony. The function of mindfulness is that it brings sufficient calmness and clarity for us to cultivate the inner qualities that lead to happiness and well-being and to understand and let go of the qualities that lead to confusion and disharmony.

Mindfulness of Feeling

Awareness of feeling is a significant aspect of mindfulness meditation. The world of our emotions is one that can be charged and unpredictable. It is a territory that often feels inaccessible to us. Within the world of emotions is carried our griefs, sorrows, disappointments, anger, love and joy. With mindfulness we learn to penetrate this complex territory understanding that every emotion is a tapestry involving our bodies, minds, feelings and frequently all of our associations from the past. Rather than being caught in our reactions or the turmoil of our emotions mindfulness brings us closer to that point where our emotional life begins to emerge. We learn to listen, accept and to bring balance and kind attentiveness into the process of feeling, without becoming entangled in reactions.

Mindfulness of Mind

Mindfulness is directed to more clearly understand all of the activities and qualities of our minds. As we first attempt to bring mindfulness into the movements of our minds we can initially feel bewildered by the complexity and busyness of our minds. As we deepen in our capacity to be mindfully attentive one moment at a time the mind will begin to slow down allowing us to perceive its true nature. We see that the mind is comprised of several distinct aspects and activities. There are the objects or contents of our

55

minds – thoughts, images, memories, ideas – which are constantly changing, often arriving unbidden and disappearing only to be replaced by yet another thought or image. There are also the different states of mind which can last longer and which often in turn condition the contents that arise. Depression, anxiety, sadness, dullness, excitement are all states of mind which have the capacity to colour our perceptions of ourselves and the moment. There are also the activities of the mind that compel us into action – the varying reactions of aversion or clinging, reflective elements, intentions are all taking place within this same territory we call the mind. Mindfulness enables us to penetrate the apparent complexity of the mind and see it in its different aspects and functions.

As we practise in meditation we will inevitably meet the often tumultuous life of our minds: the seemingly bottomless stream of thoughts that can dominate our perception of reality; the endless range of thoughts we can have about past, present and future. As we meditate we may even be tempted to conclude that it creates more thinking than occurred prior to meditation. What is actually happening is that we are simply becoming more aware of the life of our minds. Mindfulness meditation is not an exercise of thought eradication. Thought is not an obstacle to meditation; the obstacle lies in the obsessiveness, resistance or indulgence we can bring to our thinking processes. Mindfulness enables us to let go of these extra layers with which we can surround our thoughts, paving the way for thinking to be creative, clear and insightful. Through mindfulness, bringing clear, calm attention to each moment, we are revealed to ourselves without judgement or conclusion. Mindfulness strips away the confusing layers of resistance, struggle and prejudice which can make our inner landscape inaccessible to us. There is the possibility of deep and transforming insight.

Universal Story

The second area of understanding to which mindfulness is directed we may call the universal story. It is understanding the universal principles of existence that apply not only to us, but to all life. It is a dimension of understanding that takes us beyond the boundaries of our personal worlds and forges a deeper sense of interconnectedness with all life. In this expansion of understanding we are able to bring a wider and deeper perspective of exploring our own inner worlds rather than being so deeply entangled in the details and issues of our momentary experiences.

Impermanence

One of the principles to which mindfulness is directed is a direct and immediate understanding of the nature of change. Intellectually we nod wisely and knowingly when we hear the message, in all spiritual traditions, that all things are impermanent; that whatever is born will also die, whatever appears will also pass. The experiences of our lives constantly teach us about impermanence, yet it can be one of the most difficult areas of understanding to integrate deeply. In moments of pain or struggle we become enthusiastic advocates of the teaching of impermanence; we want difficult situations to end, we want to be parted from people we struggle with or dislike. In moments of pleasure, excitement or attainment we tend to develop bouts of amnesia; in the excitement of new attainments, delightful experiences or relationships of closeness we tend to forget that even all of this is not exempt from the natural rhythms of change that are intrinsic to all life.

The understanding of change can be direct and experiential; it is an understanding, which on this level can radically transform our lives.

As our understanding of changes deepens we are inclined to live more simply, to let go with greater ease and to bring a more profound quality of acceptance and ease into the inevitable changes that occur in our lives. With a deepening of our insight into impermanence comes a capacity to live our lives fully and in harmony with the way life actually is.

As we bring mindfulness into our perceptions of our body, feelings, mind and the whole tapestry of impressions we receive from the world, what we experience is constant change that we cannot control or prevent. Our bodies age, go through illness, become frail and die. What we love in one moment we may come to hate in the next. Our excitement turns to depression, our anger to forgiveness, our interest to boredom. A judgement or conclusion that appears so convincing in one moment is questioned in the next. Thoughts appear in our minds like an endless stream of sparks, arising and disappearing. Just as our inner world is constantly undergoing change, it is an essential principle of all life – here too there is minimal control or predictability. People come and go in our lives, there is union and separation. We experience gain and loss, praise and blame, success and failure, beauty and ugliness. All of life swims together in this sea of change.

Without understanding we frequently feel ourselves to be a victim of the unpredictability of life. We may struggle to create order, guarantees and certainty but in doing so we are hiding from one of life's most fundamental truths. When we reject the flow of life we live in conflict, suffering not because of the nature of life but because of the depth of our attachments and resistances. When we understand deeply the nature of life we learn to live in harmony with it. Accepting, seeing clearly, bringing balance are all aspects of mindfulness practice.

As our practice of mindfulness deepens so too does our understanding of the nature of change. Increasingly we are established in an attentiveness that is steady and unwavering, clearly perceiving the subtle arising and passing held within our experience. We understand that there is nothing that is solid, lasting that can offer to us a sanctuary from life. In the light of this understanding we are increasingly less inclined to try to grasp or preserve anything at all but to let go with ease and grace. We learn to live in harmony with the way things actually are, being fully present with and responsive to all things but holding onto nothing. With this ease of being that emerges there come true depths of sensitivity, appreciation and clarity of vision.

The Nature of Discontent

Every meditative tradition is represented as a path or a journey; a seeking for happiness, oneness and freedom. What motivates anyone to undertake this journey is some level of awareness of discontent, unease or lack of fulfilment in their current life, their way of seeing or the quality of their relationships. A core element within every tradition is to bring about the end of suffering in all its many forms – the suffering of separateness, greed, fear, limitation, conflict and struggle. Understanding the nature of all of these forms of discontent also plays a central role in all meditative traditions.

Meditation is not a rejection of life with its tapestry of pain and pleasure, nor does it attempt to serve as an anaesthetic, numbing us to life. Meditation is not an escape from life, but an understanding of it. There is a whole range of pain and suffering that none of us can avoid – grief, loss, illness and death. There is also a whole realm of suffering and struggle born of confusion and misunderstanding. It is here that there is an urgent need for us to deepen in understanding.

WAY of

Part of mindfulness practice is to bring about the end of conflict, unease and struggle born of confusion and misperception.

Cultivating a clear awareness of the nature of suffering in all of its many forms is a central theme in all traditions. This awareness is not intended to lead us to blame or despair, but to motivate us to seek compassion and the end of suffering. Poverty, violence, hunger, homelessness and loneliness are obvious levels of suffering that affect countless people. Meditation is not a withdrawal from the actualities of our world, but a compassionate opening to them. There are subtler levels of discontent and unease that exist not only in our external worlds, but that we carry within ourselves in patterns of anger, fear or alienation. Here too mindfulness is brought, not as a means of dwelling in discontent but as a means of understanding the nature of discontent and discovering the pathways which will lead to the end of conflict and struggle. There is much discontent and sorrow that is born out of not deeply understanding and accepting the intrinsically unreliable and uncertain nature of life. Dissatisfaction becomes a powerfully compelling force in our lives as we search for reliability, security and predictability outside of ourselves in attainments, possessions or people. Experiencing loss, resentment and frustration when we do not find the certainty we seek for can become a fuel for even greater restlessness. We live in a changing and fragile world and security is only illusory.

Mindfulness can transform our relationship to this changing world that carries both pain and pleasure. Instead of fleeing from or fearing pain and endlessly pursuing and trying to capture whatever appears to offer pleasure and promises of safety and satisfaction, we learn to open to and understand what is actually occurring in each moment. We begin to see not only the truth of each moment but the ways in which both avoidance and grasping create suffering for us. In meditation we may well experience peaceful and joyful states that inspire and delight us. We will also experience moments in which we are deeply aware of the dimensions of discontent we carry within us. There is no rejection of these places. In the midst of the challenging and disturbing we learn not only about the nature and causes of suffering but also the pathways to its end through balance, understanding and compassion.

Selflessness

All meditation traditions point to a discovery of a way of being, an understanding of reality far vaster than that which is defined by our minds, bodies and perceptions. The words that are used to describe this awakening vary – Godhead, Ultimate Truth, Enlightenment, Original Nature – all point to a dimension of being in which there is profound freedom. Mindfulness meditation holds awakening at its heart. Part of this awakening is discovering a profound understanding of selflessness. There are mistaken ideas in existence that believe that meditation attempts to eradicate the ego or annihilate the self – meditation does not endeavour to do this. It is a journey to discover what is true and what is false in the notions of self we carry, just as in any other dimension of our experience. We can carry with us in our lives a belief in a self, which is perceived as solid, substantial and separate from everything else. This idea of self is a composite of our beliefs, opinions, conclusions; our body, mind and personality; our memories from the past and our hopes for the future. Our notion of self has boundaries and descriptions which we seek to protect and yet at the same time feel limited by. It is a familiar territory which provides identity and ways of responding, yet it is equally the territory which fosters the pain of separateness, fear and self-consciousness.

The solidity of the notion of self is maintained through the process of identifying with the variety of events that occur in our body-mind process. By identifying with a thought, a feeling, a possession we are able to say 'I am', 'I have' and 'I know'. Mindfulness is brought to explore these moments of identifying and the semblance of solidity begins to dissolve. We penetrate beneath the layer of concept and experience directly seeing, hearing, thinking, feeling and touching. Much of our experience is not chosen or selected – thoughts, sounds, sensations and sights arise because of conditions. We don't tell our ears to hear, nor can we tell our bodies to experience a selected sensation. That which we tend to think of as 'me' or 'mine' is a changing flow of experience. There is 'no-one' who is separate from that flow, no controlling centre, no director of operations. The insight that lies at the core of this discovery is that none of the processes we call 'self' – body, feelings, perceptions, reactions or mind – are enduring or solid. Our idea of 'self' changes in accord with whatever process is most predominant and identified with. We say I am angry, sick, excited, bored – what we are describing is a changing notion of self determined by what has been isolated and identified with in our changing world. This is an understanding to be known experientially.

As we deepen in meditation our awareness of this becomes increasingly subtle on a moment-to-moment level. We are less tempted to draw conclusions about ourselves or to accept our belief systems so readily. We feel less inclined to be judgmental inwardly or outwardly. We are more easily able to be present within the flow of our experience without interference and to let go of the variety of images and descriptions through which we describe ourselves. We begin to have glimpses of a vaster way of being in which there is profound joy and peace.

Mindfulness meditation is a deepening understanding of the nature of our inner and outer life. Acceptance, balance, calmness and immediacy of seeing lay the foundations for insight to emerge. The purpose of insight is to transform and to liberate – it is a natural unfoldment, not requiring will-power or forcing but requiring only the simple, mindful attending to each moment.

Awakening

The last area of understanding which lies at the heart of mindfulness meditation and all meditative tradition is the profound understanding of freedom, awakening, liberation. This mystical dimension of meditation cannot be guaranteed by any particular technique or form. Deep levels of awakening involve a finely balanced interplay of inner commitment, effort, attentiveness, stillness and receptivity. Bringing mindfulness to understand the true nature of our inner and outer worlds is a way of laying the foundations of cultivating an inner environment of serenity, wakefulness and clarity that is deeply receptive to profound and liberating wisdom.

The Practice of Mindfulness

Mindfulness meditation has been formulated in a vast variety of different styles that range from a choiceless awareness that is brought to every posture, moment and event, to finely structured forms and styles of meditation that are systematically developed in more cloistered, formal situations and postures. There are styles of mindfulness that encourage a natural contemplation cultivated within the context of all activities – whether in formal meditation or in the activities of daily life, just as there are intensive styles of

mindfulness that advocate deep experiential insight. The key principles of cultivating calmness, clarity, receptivity and understanding
run though all of this array of practices. The delight of mindfulness
meditation lies in its portability and flexibility – every moment and
every situation is the right moment and situation to be clearly
present and mindful.

It is not possible to cover in detail every style of mindfulness meditation, but I will attempt to portray a few of the most widely practised traditions. There are many that will not be mentioned and this
is in no way ignoring them or dismissing their importance. There is
available a variety of literature that describes the numerous techniques of mindfulness meditation.

The principles previously mentioned regarding posture, quietness
and approach all apply to developing mindfulness meditation in a
formal meditation period. Taking a period of time on a daily basis
that is dedicated to cultivating the practice is invaluable. Different
styles of mindfulness meditation will adopt one specific aspect
of our inner experience as the primary focus through which the
qualities of attentiveness, clear perception and letting go are
developed. Other styles will from the beginning include all of the
dimensions of our inner world. The principles of developing
calmness, understanding and steadiness of mind run through all
the variety of styles.

Mindfulness of Body

After adopting a posture that is relaxed, alert and still, become
aware of the entire body and the variety of sensations within
it. The attention is then brought to focus upon the top of the head,
cultivating a direct and immediate perception of what is occurring

in that area. From the top of the head the attention is systematically moved down through the entire body to the tip of the toes. In this passage of attention through the body no attempt is made to conceptualize the experience nor to make anything special happen. The intention is simply to bring mindful attention into the body, acknowledging the variety of sensations that comprise the life of our bodies. Both the presence and absence of sensation is noticed; the pleasant, unpleasant and neutral sensations within the body are given an equality of attention; the way in which the various sensations are arising, passing and changing is acknowledged with sensitivity and balance. In the beginning there may only be a superficial perception of the body and the grosser sensations within it – areas of pain or tension, heat or cold or simply a basic perception of the different parts of our body.

As mindfulness deepens there comes an increasing subtlety within the perception of the body. There is mindfulness not only of the sensations within the body but also of our relationship to them. There is a deepening awareness of the ways in which we react: the holding and grasping to the pleasant sensations, the aversions, resistances or fears that may arise in relationship to the unpleasant and the inclination to slip into fantasy or numbness when in contact with sensation that is more neutral.

The practice is developed through continually, steadily moving the attention through the body, from the head to the toes, without lingering upon or avoiding any area because of the presence of pleasant or unpleasant sensations. The extremes of sensation within the body of tightness or tension release and there comes into being an evenness, calmness and vibrational level of sensation. The attention is expanded at this point simply to embrace the entire body in the light of mindfulness. Sensations subtly change, their arising and passing is noticed – the attention rests in a clear and direct perception of each moment.

As the practice develops there emerges a greater equanimity and steadiness within the consciousness and the ability to embrace the world of feeling and sensation without preference. There is a deeply enhanced understanding of the nature of change and non-solidity within the body. Calmness and happiness strengthen as the mind is no longer dominated by the pull and push of sensation, preferences and reactions.

In this style of mindfulness meditation, the body is seen to provide a microcosmic view of life. The principles of change and selflessness seen on a moment-to-moment level within the body are the fundamental principles of all life. The changing experiences of pleasure, pain and neutral sensation are found within every dimension of our lives. Undoing through mindfulness our conditioned reactions of being for and against, fear or grasping, not only changes our inner relationship but is a growing understanding that impacts upon our entire life bringing understanding, happiness and balance.

Mindfulness with Bare Attention

In this frequently used style of mindfulness meditation the attention is brought initially to focus upon the breathing either at the entrance to the nostrils or in the rising and falling of the abdomen. The breath provides the primary focus point or anchor within each moment but no attempt is made to exclude anything else. From the point of attentiveness mindfulness is brought to see clearly each moment the attention is drawn away from the breath to a sound, body sensation, feeling or thought. Bare attention is brought to these moments, they are not considered to be distractions, but equally warranting bare attention to simply see them as they are – a thought as a thought, a sound as a sound, a sensation as a sensation. No judgement is made, nothing is added or subtracted, no attempt to analyse where they arose from or why they are present is engaged in – there is just seeing. When no extra layers of preference, reaction or judgement are added all of these dimensions of our experience arise and also pass away. There is no intention to linger anywhere, but simply to be clearly present with whatever is predominant in our experience in each moment with bare attention and then to return to the primary focal point of the breath.

Bringing bare attention we see what is occurring in each moment and our responses. The layers of habit, reaction and inattention begin to fall away. On a moment-to-moment level we see where struggle and discontent is created through misperception and confusion and we see the pathways to letting go of struggle. Our capacity to perceive each moment just as it is becomes increasingly subtle and a deeper understanding of the true nature of each moment emerges. Struggle and its cause, the nature of change and a clearer understanding of selflessness are all insights born of an immediate, clear and balanced mindfulness.

Bare Attention with Noting

This style of mindfulness meditation is cultivated in a similar manner to the above practice but with an added ingredient – that of simply naming each moment of perception. The attention is again primarily focused within the breath at the abdomen or entrance to the nostrils. In harmony with the natural movement of the breath a name or label is used to clarify what is actually taking place. If the breath is focused in the abdomen, 'rising' with the inbreath and 'falling' with the outbreath is used. If the attention is focused in the area of the nose, then the note 'in breath' or 'out breath' is used with each inhalation and each exhalation.

The same process of noting is brought to all of the moments when our attention is drawn away from the breath. The noting is used with great simplicity in order to clarify each of our perceptions and inner movements. 'Thinking', 'hearing', 'feeling' are joined to the predominant movement of the mind. The noting is intended to cultivate an attention that is clear and close to each moment of perception. As the mindfulness deepens the noting also becomes more precise – to acknowledge more specific themes within our perceptions. Thought is noted as 'fantasy', 'memory', 'planning', etc, to clearly perceive what is happening in the moment. Sounds that present themselves are noted simply with 'hearing' or 'listening', 'harsh' or 'soft'. Sensation is more clearly noted as 'pain' or 'pleasure'. The noting is not habitual or mechanical but is a tool to bring us closer to the moment, to cultivate a clearer understanding of what is taking place within us. In deeper levels of mindfulness the noting becomes unnecessary as there is a direct and immediate perception of each moment as it occurs, and the noting naturally falls away.

As in all styles of mindfulness meditation the core of this practice is the development of wisdom. Rooted in the present moment, freeing us of habitual patterns, seeing deeply into each moment and understanding the essential nature of all events and movements.

Mindfulness with Investigation

Again in this style of mindfulness the attention is initially brought to rest in the primary anchor, the breath. A specific intention is brought into the meditation which will focus upon clearly comprehending the dynamics of our inner experience. These intentions can vary, but a single intention should be adopted for at least the duration of a single sitting – the intention is often explored over much longer periods of time. We can begin our meditation with intention to notice beginnings and endings in all of the movements in our inner experience – beginnings and endings of the breath, thoughts, sensations or sounds. We can bring the intention to notice movements of either resistance or grasping within these aspects of our experience. The intention to notice the feeling tone of pleasant, unpleasant or neutral within the sounds, thoughts, or sensations that present themselves can be brought. The introduction of this intentional element into our meditation is designed to bring a greater sense of precision and clear comprehension into our meditation. The noticing is undertaken in the spirit of bare attention and simplicity – no conclusions are drawn nor is there any need to add extra layers of thinking or comparison.

Mindfulness of Space

In many of the styles of mindfulness meditation the primary emphasis is upon the changing objects of our experience as they present themselves with the intention of cultivating the principles of clarity of perception, calmness and understanding. In this style of mindfulness meditation the emphasis is not upon the objects that arise and pass but upon the space in which they appear and disappear. It is like looking at the sky without isolating the clouds or stars, focusing instead upon the vastness of the sky which holds them. It is a way of listening inwardly and outwardly in which the objects that appear are secondary in significance – it is going beneath the objects to connect more deeply with the consciousness which embraces and receives everything. As calmness and clarity deepen there grows an increasing capacity to rest within the profound peace and stillness of this non-judgmental, non-preferential spaciousness – open to receiving everything that arises yet not seeking anything in particular.

Initially this perception of space takes place in the form of brief glimpses – we notice the pause of space between the end of one breath and the beginning of another, the space between thoughts, sounds and sensations. As inner calmness develops we begin to perceive not only the space between the sounds, thoughts, feelings and sensations that arise and pass, but also the greater stillness and space in which they appear. It is a perception born of balance, tranquillity and the understanding that frees us of the points of reference which imprison us in habitual reactions.

Mindfulness in Daily Life

It is during our formal periods of meditation that we learn the skills and the art of attentiveness, mindfulness, simplicity and understanding – the essential principles of mindfulness meditation. These skills can be translated into every activity in our lives to bring clarity, calm and wisdom and it is necessary that this translation takes place. Any meditation will have only limited value if it is solely confined to a particular posture or time. Meditation is intended to transform the whole of our lives and if it is to fulfil this intention it needs to be applied in every moment and every circumstance. We do not need a special time or place to be mindful – these times support and strengthen our capacity to answer the invitation of every moment to be present, clear and attentive.

When our bodies are in motion, whether driving our car, eating or walking, we are offered choices. We can spend those moments planning our next activity, reminiscing about the past or daydreaming, or we can bring a mindful attentiveness into those movements cultivating oneness, simplicity and sensitivity. Being wholeheartedly where we are, fully with what we are doing is the essence of mindfulness.

Because of the familiarity of many of our regular daily activities we tend to overlook or dismiss them as moments undeserving of mindfulness, yet it is often within these activities that we become most habitual, prone to dullness or reaction. These are also the places we learn to be awake, sensitive and integrated with whatever is taking place. Bringing wholehearted mindfulness to each moment infuses it with vitality and life. We clearly perceive the beginnings and endings in all things, being present we are enriched through appreciation, being focused we are less prone to accumulating so many of the mental residues that result from a scattered attentiveness in our lives. In the development of mindfulness, 'what' we are doing or engaged in is of secondary significance – the quality of our presence in each moment is of primary significance. Mindfulness awakens us, bringing oneness, calmness and understanding.

Further specific applications of mindfulness are explored in Chapter 6, 'Meditation in Daily Life'.

FOUR

DEVOTION

In every great spiritual tradition there is found the principle of devotion. Devotion is the most frequently practised style of meditation in our contemporary world. Tibetan Buddhists reciting mantras on their malas (prayer beads), Sufis dancing, Hasidic Jews meeting in prayer in a synagogue and Christians joining their voices in hymn or gathering together in silent prayer are all engaged in practices of devotion even though the objects of their veneration may differ. The countless differing rituals of offerings, festivals of thanksgiving and forms of adoration found within every spiritual tradition serve as vehicles for expressing devotion. Devotional practices provide the opportunity to express gratitude and love – they are a celebration of the divine or sacred essence of all traditions.

Devotional meditation may be undertaken in silence or vocalized through chants or prayers; it may involve physical stillness or be expressed in the movement of dance or bowing; it may be cultivated in solitude or a collective activity of celebration and adoration. In all of these different forms the heart, mind and body are unified and directed towards a transcendental realization and understanding of oneness. The essence of all devotional practices is love – initially focused externally but expanding to be an all-encompassing love. In theistic traditions devotion is directed towards a spiritual deity or entity, providing a focus for reverence, love, gratitude and trust. In non-theistic traditions such as Buddhism devotion is cultivated through ritual and reflection that clarifies the aspirations for awakening, compassion and understanding the devotee is seeking to foster in their own heart and mind. Initially in non-theistic traditions an external subject such as a deity, spiritual figure or awakened teacher is chosen as the focus for devotional direction. In every tradition devotion provides the focus and forms where individuals can gather, finding support in collective meditation and celebration, often balancing the solitariness of their individual spiritual paths.

The principles and goals of devotional practice are purity of heart and mind, joy, transcendental love, selflessness and ultimately a profound and mystical experience of union or communion with the subject to which devotion is extended. Devotional meditation involves a celebration of the presence of the divine or transcendent, a cultivation of love and commitment and an unwavering attentiveness. The principles of effort, discipline and patience found in other meditative styles are equally highlighted in the path of devotion.

The primary inner qualities which are highlighted and developed in devotional practices of meditation are faith, energy, concentration and surrender. These form the core principles of all forms of devotional meditation. In theistic traditions these qualities are developed in relationship to a divine figure or entity initially seen to be separate and apart from the devotee. In non-theistic traditions these inner qualities are fostered in relationship to an image or spiritual figure, such as the buddha, that symbolizes ultimate reality, purity of heart and mind and awakening – realizations that are also perceived initially to be separate from the devotee.

Devotional practices always begin from a place of separateness or duality where the devotee feels apart and removed from the subject of veneration and devotion. Devotion is a path of going beyond the self; of dissolving this separation – reaching a point of realization where the separate self is submerged in the divine or mystical figure or quality that has previously been adored from afar. Devotional practices are a path of reaching for a greater, vaster sense of reality and being – initially symbolized by the subject of devotion – ultimately found within the devotee. The external object of devotion ultimately leads devotees back to themselves; to discover that the qualities and realizations previously felt to be inherent in the external deity or entity, are actually immanent within themselves, awakened by their love and one-pointedness. The sense of separation between the devotee and the subject of devotion is dissolved by the devotional practice and transformed into communion and oneness. As devotional meditation deepens the interpersonal love first felt by the devotee towards the deity or figure changes to a transcendental quality of love that is universal and all-embracing. The states of joy, oneness and happiness once evoked through focusing upon the deity or figure become a natural part of the devotee's own consciousness and being. Oneness, communion, non-separateness and love are the guiding principles of all devotional styles.

Key Principles in Devotion

Concentration

One key principle that devotional practices share with all other styles of meditation is the emphasis upon concentration or one-pointedness. A finely focused, steady attentiveness is fundamental to deepening in any style of meditation including devotion. The quality of transcendental oneness that is ultimately sought in devotional meditation, begins with forming a stable bond of oneness, through attention, with the chosen subject of devotion, whether it is a mantra, visual symbol, prayer or divine entity. The subject of devotion is chosen and the mind is collected and focused upon it, both in formal meditation and in all the activities of one's day – the attention is repeatedly turned towards the mantra, prayer or visual symbol. Through this focusing the habit of remembrance becomes more powerful than all of the other mental habits of the devotee such as fantasy, distractedness or dwelling in past or future. The mantra, prayer, symbol or figure becomes central in the mind and heart, it is kept foremost through the power of the atten-tiveness that develops. Through the love and faith which are also ingredients of devotion the mind will gradually become increasing-ly engaged with the object of devotion, other thoughts and habits will decrease in their power to attract one's interest and will simply come and go on the periphery of consciousness.

Similar phases of development occur in concentration when it is utilized in devotional practices as when concentration is used solely to develop single-pointedness. Initially the mind will be tempted, through habit and distractedness, to wander away from the mantra, prayer or symbol that has been chosen. The attention may feel weak or wavering, often the object of focus will be forgotten or lost in the whirlwind of thoughts, images and memories that stream through the mind. The same principles of concentration, as previously discussed, apply here. Concentration requires patience and the consistent will-ingness to begin again in each moment. Through these qualities attention will begin to deepen and steady as it is continually returned to the present moment and the chosen focus of attention. There will gradually come a greater sense of ease in staying close to the chosen object of focus, it will become more vivid and tangible and eventual-ly become a natural resting place of the mind. The attention becomes increasingly effortless as the happiness of attentiveness and the joy of oneness is discovered. As the richness, ease and well-being of atten-tion are discovered the mind becomes increasingly less inclined towards the habits of distractedness and superficiality.

As this occurs the mind will begin to calm and quiet. Agitation and restlessness will be replaced by a deeper sense of happiness and well-being felt in both mind and body. These states in themselves can ripen with further development into profound states of rapture and bliss. As this deepening occurs the more tangible object of concentration such as the mantra or symbol will recede and eventually drop away. The attention becomes powerful enough that it no longer needs the reminder of the concentration subject in order to stay focused. The attention begins to be absorbed into the object of devotion, the sense of separation decreases and eventually the whole consciousness and body is saturated with sublime joy and a profound sense of oneness with the object of devotion.

Concentration is one aspect of devotional practice – it is where we begin. It is a training that requires dedication, time, patience and effort. Calmness in our approach is essential if calmness is to be realized. It is, however, concentration that allows the other key principles of devotion to ripen and be realized. Once concentration is established, devotional practices diverge from other styles of meditation to reveal their own unique characteristics.

Faith

Faith is a primary principle that inspires us to embark on every journey we make in our lives, whether it is an attempt to scale a mountain or undertake a spiritual path. Within every journey we begin we move from the familiar to the unfamiliar, from the known to the unknown. A spiritual path begins with establishing our attention in our present reality and moves towards the fulfilment of aspirations and possibilities not yet realized. Awakening, compassion, love and understanding are the qualities and goals we seek to awaken through our meditation practice. Faith is the quality of heart and mind that includes confidence, courage, love, openness and commitment, all qualities necessary in the journey we make of discovery and transformation. Faith provides the inspiration and encouragement to reach beyond the boundaries of what is known and familiar to us and reach for greatness of heart and spirit.

Every spiritual practice will ask of us the willingness to question and explore all aspects of our lives – our beliefs, opinions, images and assumptions – and to open to new understandings and discoveries. The softening and opening of our hearts and minds is an organic and natural aspect of meditation practice. In this opening it is possible that many of our previously cherished conclusions, values and perceptions will be transformed. Change happens not through resolution or will-power but through understanding and experience. On a moment-to-moment level we become increasingly aware of the forces in our minds and lives that lead to alienation and unhappiness and the qualities that lead to understanding and peace. Meditation will not take anything away from us, but through meditation there will be a natural falling away of the untrue or questionable in the light of understanding and attention. The stillness, calmness and receptivity of meditation allow us to see with greater clarity and depth and there is nothing that is exempt from this, including the conclusions, beliefs or images we may hold about ourselves.

Faith provides the courage, commitment and confidence that enable us to participate fully in this process of discovery; it is a pillar of transformation. Faith balances the many doubts that will arise as we engage in meditation – doubts about our progress, our ability to deepen and awaken, the validity of the path we have chosen and the possibility of its fulfilment. Doubt can be a paralysing force in any meditative journey if it is met with dismissiveness or negativity. Doubt can also be an enlivening and inspiring force if it returns us to the present moment with a greater openness and willingness to explore ourselves more deeply.

Faith is different from belief – it does not involve possessing an unassailable collection of convictions, opinions or certainties. The quality of faith that sustains us on a meditative journey is not blind or narrow, but open and receptive. Genuine faith asks us to look again and again at our path in the light of our own experience. The acid test of any meditative style is whether it works for us in our lives. Does it lead to happiness, calmness and understanding? Is it bringing about changes in ourselves and in our lives that manifest in deeper clarity, well-being and balance.

There are two key directions held within every manifestation of faith. Faith is clearly directed towards the subject of devotion that embodies or symbolizes our aspirations for oneness and awakening. The symbol or figure of our devotion represents the unknown, the goal, the fulfilment of our longings for oneness, happiness and wisdom. The other direction of faith is towards ourselves. Through our meditation practice and experience we learn to have confidence in ourselves and our own possibilities of awakening and realization. The bridge between ourselves and our goal, the realization of oneness and awakening is our path, the meditative practice we are engaged in.

Faith is a quality that undergoes a number of changes in accord with the way in which our experience deepens and changes. There is an element of faith present in everyone who embarks on a spiritual path. This initial faith may be wavering or vague, co-existing with doubt. It is not uncommon to feel a deep sense of faith in our practice and ourselves when our meditation experience is joyous and deep, only to find that our faith dissipates in the light of challenging or dry times in our meditation. In the beginning of meditation we are tempted to evaluate our practice in terms of 'success' and 'failure'. Calmness, stillness and concentration are interpreted as the signposts of 'success'. Agitation, distractedness or dullness are interpreted as the signposts of 'failure'. As we mature in our meditation practice there develops a more stable faith and confidence that is not so swayed by the ups and downs of our experience. Our delight in 'success' and our despair over 'failure' are replaced by a more balanced willingness to meet whatever is occurring in each moment with a willingness to learn. The fragile faith we bring to the first steps of our practice is fostered and strengthened through the practice of devotion.

Reflection

Devotional practices hold within them an element of reflection and contemplation. Whether the devotion is directed towards a divine entity or the possibility of enlightenment reflection is a calm, focused contemplation and appreciation of the qualities of wisdom, compassion and love embodied in and symbolized by the focus of our devotion. Through reflection and ritual a heartfelt longing for oneness and communion is awakened in our hearts that plays a major role in strengthening our capacity to stay concentrated upon the focus of our devotion. Reflection is one element of awakening love, dedication and energy within ourselves. Through reflection we explore what universal compassion, selflessness and generosity means for us and the difference that the presence of these qualities would make in our lives. Through reflection the symbol of our devotion, with all its attributes, increasingly stays foremost in our attention, our minds begin to steady and our capacity for attentiveness and recollection deepens. In the light of this experience our faith in ourselves grows and strengthens as we see directly our capacity for calmness, happiness and one-pointedness being realized. Authentic spiritual practices do not call for blind faith, but for the confidence, steadiness and trust that are rooted in and validated by the reality of our own experience. As our experience deepens and expands, so too does our faith in the direction of our devotion and in our own capacity for realization.

Purity

The theme of purity is one that runs through all spiritual traditions. Purity of conduct, heart and mind are presented as being the foundation for depth in any spiritual practice. It is a theme that is particularly highlighted in devotional practice. The focus of devotion whether it wears the name of God, the Divine or True Nature symbolizes the ultimate purity of heart and mind the devotee is aspiring to. Universal happiness, wisdom, compassion and joy are all aspects of this purity that the devotee is encouraged to reflect upon as a means to awakening these qualities within themselves. The principles of service, generosity, ritual and meditation found in all traditions are presented as the ways of awakening these qualities immanent within the devotee.

Purity of conduct represented in the ethical guidelines, precepts and commandments of every tradition is a way of refraining from actions and speech that lead to harm, conflict and divisiveness and provide a way of conduct that leads to respect, appreciation and sensitivity. They are undertaken as a training and practice that lead us to find greater depths of kindness, care and compassion within ourselves. Purity of mind and heart is found through accepting and understanding the unskilful and divisive – yet not engaging in the habits of greed, anger and selfishness that can easily dominate our hearts and minds. Through holding foremost in our attention the qualities of the divine: compassion, boundless love and wisdom, we are encouraged to forsake the pathways of self-centeredness and seek to discover in ourselves a way of being that emulates the sacred.

The cultivation of purity of conduct, heart and mind is not in order to achieve a stature of superiority or self-righteousness. There is a wisdom element within the cultivation of purity – the clear acknowledgement that greed, anger and selfishness deny happiness, openness and oneness and that generosity, honesty, care and compassion lead directly to joy, understanding and well-being for ourselves and others. The qualities of purity initially invested in the focus of devotion are awakened within the heart and mind of the devotee through dedication and practice. In devotional practices the devotee is constantly aspiring to find union with the focus of devotion and all its attributes. It is a practice of letting go of the limiting, the habits that bind the devotee to separateness and unhappiness and a reaching for the vastness of joy and freedom represented by the focus of devotion. The distance between the devotee and the focus of devotion is lessened and dissolved through the efforts of the devotee to cultivate one-pointedness, purity and wisdom.

Selflessness

A profound understanding of selflessness is central to devotional styles of meditation, just as it is a principle found within all schools of meditation. The inevitable result of thinking of ourselves in a limited way, defined by our bodies, minds and personalities, is separation and isolation. Separation and isolation are furthered by all of the activities of self, as we assert or defend our sense of self through conclusions, opinions, anger, greed and fear. All paths of meditation, through different means, will challenge and question the beliefs and assumptions we hold about ourselves and will invite us to transform greed, hatred and alienation through love and understanding. All paths of meditation will invite us to seek what is true, rather than accepting the confinement of limited images and conclusions about ourselves.

Devotion seeks selflessness through recollection, one-pointedness, purity and surrender. The devotee's attention is constantly and repeatedly turned towards the symbol of devotion and there is in this recollection a withdrawal from entanglement with other pursuits in the world and patterns of preoccupation. The primary interest and focus in all moments and activities of the devotee is keeping the symbol of their devotion alive in their attention and heart. The guiding principle in all activities is not what is in the service of self-interest but what serves the fulfilment of love, purity and compassion. Purity of conduct brings with it the well-being and ease of mind that allows the attention to be sustained. The mind is less entangled in the residues of guilt and remorse that are left by self-centred activity.

As the attention becomes increasingly focused on the subject of devotion there is a natural surrendering of many of the activities and preoccupations of self-interest such as greed, anger, prestige and anxiety, as the consciousness becomes increasingly saturated with attention to and love of the focus of devotion. Increasingly the activities and demands of the self are seen as being transparent and questionable. Joy and love for the subject of devotion become the dominant characteristics of the consciousness. The attributes and qualities of the subject of devotion increasingly become the awakened qualities of the devotee. The devotee begins to perceive the divine in all things, everything becomes sacred and an embodiment of the divine. The sense of separation, previously sparked by the activities and belief in a limited self, dissolves and the sacred is perceived in all things. Selflessness is a natural culmination of the surrender of separation.

Devotional Practices

The styles of devotion will vary in different traditions, yet the principles of one-pointedness, reflection, purity and selflessness remain constant.

Mantras

The use of mantras is one of the most frequently found styles of devotional practice, encountered in a range of spiritual traditions that include Christianity, Buddhism and Hinduism. A mantra may be a single syllable or sound that represents the transcendental qualities of the divine or limitless consciousness. Different traditions use a range of mantras, such as 'Hare Krishna', 'Namo Buddhia', 'Kyrie Eleison', 'God is love', 'Lord Jesus Christ, have mercy on me', or 'Om mane padme hum'. The mantra may be composed of a single phrase taken from the scriptures that represents to the devotee the fulfilment of their aspiration to be awakened and liberated. It is significant that the mantra is meaningful and evocative of realization to the devotee, so that the repetition does not become a habitual recital. The mantra is a symbol, sometimes chanted aloud, other times repeated silently. With the conscious, mindful repetition of the mantra there is both a celebration and remembrance of the attributes of the divine or transcendent. It is this quality of remembrance and reflection that makes the mantra into a devotional practice rather than purely a concentration practice.

Through repeating the mantra, slowly and consistently the attention is focused and steadied. The mantra provides a tangible place for the attention to be returned to each time the mind wanders or becomes distracted. Through practice and repetition, the mantra becomes a close companion, present in all activities and moments;

its repetition becomes instinctive and it becomes a natural resting place of the attention. The mind becomes increasingly still and calm and there begins to emerge calmness, happiness and single-pointedness. In deeper levels of practice with a mantra there is absorption into the mantra at which point the words or sound of the mantra will naturally drop away. In these states of absorption qualities of rapture, joy and bliss emerge, there is a minimal perception of body consciousness or of consciousness of anything at all outside of the qualities of the absorption. There is a deep sense of union, oneness and the qualities of the divine previously attributed to the focus of devotion are directly discovered within the consciousness of the devotee. There is a flowering of love and compassion.

Apart from the mystical experience that can be encountered through prolonged mantra practice, many devotees find it to be of tremendous value within the context of their daily lives. Mantras provide an easily accessible anchor for attentiveness in the midst of a busy life, they are a refuge from chaotic thinking or preoccupation. The mantra is also symbolic – it represents the aspirations of the devotee and provides a powerful reminder of direction and focus when habits of greed, anger or confusion arise.

Prayer

In the Christian tradition prayer is the most frequently practised style of meditation. From the earliest times of Christianity, devotees have followed the instruction to 'pray always' as a means of cultivating a deeper unity with the divine. Although less used in other traditions, prayer shares the same principle of encouraging the devotee to open their heart and mind to em-brace a vaster understanding of reality than the one perceived only through the sense doors and the mind. Prayer equally calls for the same qualities of humility, sincerity, self-discipline and ethics that form the central core of all meditation styles.

Like mantras, the practice of prayer can be undertaken silently or verbally, in solitude or in community, in formal meditation or permeating all the activities of a day. The constant remembrance of God imbues the heart and mind with love, faith and perseverance. The concentration developed through the use of prayer will bring the mind to stillness and joy as in other systems of meditation.

There are a number of different approaches to prayer. One will emphasize contemplation or reflection. A passage from the scriptures can become the focus of attention. It is read, remembered and contemplated as a way of exploring its meaning and relevance to the devotee. Contemplation may revolve around a single subject such as forgiveness, humility, faith or love and the devotee holds the subject constantly in their consciousness seeking to open their heart to a deeper understanding of what this quality means and implies. This kind of contemplation is radically different from just discursive or random thinking. Contemplation does not seek a prescribed answer or quick solution – rather it is the questioning of the meaning of love, humility or compassion, that is of greatest significance. By constantly bringing the attention back to the question gently held within the consciousness, the mind becomes more still, receptive and calm allowing for a deeper intuitive response to emerge. Other qualities of devotion such as faith, love and purity are born of the stillness and well-being that emerge from prolonged and dedicated contemplation.

One of the primary prayer practices is in the adoption of a single phrase from the scriptures that highlights a particularly meaningful quality or attribute of the divine, such as 'Make me a channel of your peace'. Prayer is used in a way similar to mantra practice – the phrase is focused upon as the primary object of attention and constantly returned to. It is repeated mindfully, with each word of the phrase concentrated on, emphasizing its meaning. It is not a mechanical recitation, but through concentrating on the meaning of each word the devotee cultivates not only concentration but also love and receptivity. The phrase provides a constant remembrance of the divine. In consistently returning the attention to the chosen phrase, the devotee excludes all other thoughts and the phrase increasingly becomes accessible, vivid and tangible. The mind gradually becomes more still and the attention more effortless. Like other styles of concentration practices the aim of this consistent focusing is absorption in the object of focus. The gap between the devotee and the object of devotion disappears, eventually even the phrase drops away and there is both stillness and joy. Concentration, however, is not the sole aim of prayer. The mystical element of this experience of oneness is deeper than just the absorption of the devotee's consciousness in the phrase. The oneness that is sought in the practice of prayer is beyond the personal ego and requires the devotee to be submerged in the will and attributes of the divine.

Visualization

Visualization is a widely practised style of meditation in a variety of spiritual traditions. Visualization practice straddles two primary principles of meditation. It is a powerful concentration practice; it also holds within it the primary qualities of devotion. When used solely as a concentration practice the object of visualization is often neutral in association, such as a candle flame or a simple picture. When visualization is used to cultivate both concentration and devotion the object of visualization will generally be a symbol, picture or deity that holds a greater spiritual significance and association for the devotee. In more advanced visualization practices the symbol or image becomes increasingly complex, demanding far greater powers of concentration and skill from the devotee.

Many visualization subjects that are chosen, represent and are seen to embody specific qualities of heart and mind that the devotee seeks to cultivate within themselves, such as wisdom, purity or compassion. Visualization is often preceded by a period of reflection dedicated to contemplating these qualities. The devotee seeks to identify with the quality as they undertake their visualization. This combination of reflection and visualization fosters not only concentration, but also faith, devotion and wisdom. The devotee seeks oneness in visualization — not only oneness of mind with the chosen focus of attention but also oneness with the qualities seen to be embodied in the visual object. Constantly recollecting the highlighted quality such as compassion or wisdom, the devotee increasingly becomes aware without condemnation of the opponents or opposites of these qualities such as anger or selfishness when they emerge within themselves. The clarity and balance of attention that has been fostered through the visualization practice enables the meditator to increasingly see clearly into these patterns of mind and to bring compassion and understanding to them. Visualization practice strongly emphasizes the wisdom element of meditation – it is not intended only to produce elevated states of concentration but also to awaken and liberate the consciousness.

Visualization practice requires periods of solitude and sustained cultivation in formal meditation. Initially a picture of the symbol or deity is placed before the meditator. A visual connection is made with the picture and it becomes familiar. Closing the eyes an attempt is then made to recall the symbol in consciousness. It can be slowly reconstructed piece by piece. When the attention is still fragile the picture is often difficult to recall or appears in a very vague way. The eyes can be reopened to make a visual connection. With practice it becomes increasingly possible to recall the symbol in consciousness with greater ease and clarity and to hold it for lengthening periods of time. As this happens there is less intrusion of other mental activities and the symbol eventually comes to occupy the whole of the consciousness. This is a deep level of concentration which continues to develop. As it does so perceptions of anything outside of the conscious symbol, such as bodily sensations, sounds and thoughts, fade away and the consciousness becomes absorbed in the image. As in any other form of concentration practice this stage of absorption is accompanied by joy, profound calmness and balance.

Visualization practices attract many people who find greater ease in developing concentration with a more tangible object such as a symbol or picture. Equally because it is a pathway that embraces devotion, concentration and wisdom it is felt by many practitioners to be a style of meditation that addresses inclusively many of their spiritual inclinations. It is helpful to remember that there is such a wide array of meditation styles simply because of the variety of temperaments within those who seek to practise meditation.

Ritual

From earliest times social and religious cultures have created a vast array of different rituals. Rituals have served many purposes – to protect communities from fear, as a means of expressing gratitude and thanksgiving, to create environments of collective worship and as a means for individuals to establish and sustain a relationship with the sacred or divine. Every spiritual tradition offers ritual in a variety of different forms as a means of cultivating faith and devotion. Participation in ritual equally provides the opportunity to form community and find support through the presence of others on similar paths. Perhaps even more importantly ritual provides a visible symbol of aspiration. Living in a world where we are constantly assailed by symbols that encourage possessiveness, acquisition, success and appearance, the symbols of wisdom, compassion and awakening emphasized through spiritual ritual become increasingly important.

Rituals assume different forms according to the tradition they are rooted in. Chants, blessings, offerings, prayers and the various rituals that mark life changes such as birth and death all serve to provide the devotee with a deep sense of connection with a tradition and teaching. The various rituals serve as symbols of deeper meaning, fostering faith, confidence and understanding. Rituals provide this sense of meaning when they are approached with sincerity, sensitivity and mindfulness. They remind us of the greater community and tradition within which we undertake our own meditative path. When a community comes together to bless and welcome a new child with flowers and prayers, to celebrate the coming of age of an adolescent, or to plant a tree in memory of someone who has died, they are strengthened in a collective intention. When you enter a meditation room and bow to your companions, you are dedicating your efforts to the well-being of all.

Many spiritual traditions hold within them complex rituals that involve chanting or singing, prayer, offerings and professions of faith. For many people these times of collective ritual are also a meditative time of stillness in their life in which they re-dedicate themselves to a path of commitment, faith, integrity and wisdom.

Rituals do not need to be complex nor will they necessarily form a part of the spiritual life of many people who aspire to profound love and wisdom. Some people find it helpful to take part in simple rituals such as lighting a candle at the beginning of a meditation period or taking a few moments at the end to dedicate their meditation to universal well-being, or to ring a bell or bow. The meaningfulness of all ritual is directly linked to the depth of heartfulness and sincerity we bring to them.

FIVE

CALMING THE
Mind and Body

Meditation is rooted in the mystical and spiritual traditions that run through all religions. Yet undertaking a meditative path is not intended to divorce us from the world but to find a greater quality of integration, calmness and understanding within all of our life. Meditation is not intended to be a means of escape from ourselves or the challenges of our life but offers a way to meet the variety of demands and interactions we encounter with skill and sensitivity. Even if we were tempted to retreat to a cave or monastery and live as a hermit, we would take with us our minds and bodies and their capacities for confusion, stress and tension as well as for serenity and clarity. The mountain-top hermit and the commuter on a train are equally concerned with discovering the pathways to calmness and peace.

Meditation is not only a mystical path but also a path of relevance and application, teaching us the way to find balance and harmony in our lives and well-being and integration within our minds and bodies. Through meditation we can learn the skills of finding calm and well-being in the midst of the stress, disappointments, illness and pain we will all inevitably meet in our lives. We can learn to heal ourselves; our bodies, minds and emotions – not through avoidance or suppression but through mindfulness and understanding. We can learn to be at home in our body, our mind and our life, free of anxiety and tension.

We live in a world which holds vast potential for stress and tension. It is a world which also, for many people, becomes full of anxiety, apprehension and confusion. Some of the challenges we meet are intrinsic to living – none of us have control over many of the events that affect our minds and bodies. Illness, pain and loss are part of the human story. They are experiences that make a powerful impression upon our minds, hearts and bodies. These changes that occur in our lives ask us to discover within ourselves deep levels of calmness and clarity so they do not turn into experiences of catastrophe and disaster that shatter us.

There are other levels of stress created through the values of our culture and the manner of our own lifestyles. The stress of deadlines, time, the numerous demands that arise from our work or lack of work; financial stress and the tensions that are born of competitiveness, ambition and the fear of failure can permeate all of our waking and sleeping moments. The relationships we are drawn to for the intimacy and warmth they offer can equally be a source of stress as we struggle with issues of acceptance and honesty. Our relationships to food, self-image, criticism and goals are all areas of potential tension and struggle. The stress that can emerge from all of these areas of our lives is experienced as anxiety, unease, tension and reactivity that affect our minds and bodies. Caught in the spiral of tension, harried by demands, we begin to find stress everywhere, becoming frustrated and reactive in the face of even small events and encounters that don't accord to our desires or timetables. If we find ourselves becoming impatient and angry with people we care for; anxious in the face of new challenges, waking in the morning with a sense of dread or greeting small disappointments with a sense of disaster, we are caught in a spiral of stress. These experiences are messengers reminding us of the need to give greater care and attention to the quality of our lives.

We frequently cannot control the events and encounters of our lives – there will be moments of disappointment and failure, times of illness and loss, times when we are unable to achieve what we want. We are however not powerless in our relationship to these experiences – in the ways that we receive and respond to the variety of challenges in our lives. Whether or not these challenges lead to

> **Checklist of Symptoms of Stress**
> 1 *Sleeplessness*
> 2 *Frequent headaches, neck pain*
> 3 *Finding ourselves overreacting to small challenges and intrusions*
> 4 *Strongly repetitive or obsessive thinking*
> 5 *Feeling of anxiety or dread, of being overwhelmed*
> 6 *Overeating, or overindulgence in alcohol, etc.*

stress, breakdown and devastation or are met with calmness and understanding has much to do with the quality of mindfulness and well-being we bring to all of the changes and demands of our lives. We cannot control life but we can powerfully influence how we meet, understand and make peace with the challenges we encounter. We can learn to cultivate an inner refuge of calmness and clarity and develop the skills of relaxation, mindfulness and well-being.

Stress is unease, discontent and tension. When we are stressed we feel very distant from any authentic quality of happiness and well-being. Caught in tension and stress we do not feel at home, at ease in our bodies or in our life. Not knowing the skills of undoing the tangles of tension within our minds and bodies we attempt to escape from and avoid the discomfort of stress in ways that frequently lead to further tension and pain. We want to get rid of the painful elements and effects of stress, not seeing that resistance to what is happening in our bodies and minds only reinforces anxiety and tension. We may attempt to disconnect ourselves from the state of our minds and bodies through overindulgence in food, alcohol, drugs or entertainment in a search for comfort and reassurance. Saturating our minds and bodies with consumption and distraction only serves to camouflage the distress we are in. It is not uncommon to see a person with every sense door engaged in consumption – eating, listening to music, reading and moving all at the same time, and call this activity relaxation.

Rather than a genuine relaxation this saturation of the sense doors tends to be a temporary reprieve from the discomfort of feeling what is actually happening in our mind and body. We return to our lives with the same patterns of mind and body, such as anxiety, confusion or ambition that create and accumulate new cycles of stress. Pursuing the path of avoidance or escape has the effect of further alienating us from our mind-body processes and escalating stress. One of the gifts of meditation practice is in teaching us the way to turn our attention directly to the stress factors in our lives and address them with calmness and sensitivity.

Meditation is not a magical cure-all for stress, but it offers a clear and transformative way of learning to respond with greater skill to the demands of our lives. It is not a path of avoidance or of instant solutions but it teaches us to turn towards the areas of stress, conflict or confusion that are present in our lives and to learn to approach them with mindfulness, acceptance and understanding. We can learn to be a conscious and active participant in cultivating the well-being of our mind and body. We can learn to foster an environment of healing within ourselves through calmness and clarity of understanding. Healing is different from curing. Meditation will make no promise to eliminate pain or cure chronic illness, but it can teach us the way of finding a sanctuary of calmness and peace within ourselves even in the midst of pain, conflict or challenge – changing our relationship to these moments in a way that we no longer feel powerless or victimized by them. The understanding we can reach through meditation and mindfulness will also teach us the ways to let go of the patterns of tension and reactivity that arise through being disconnected from our minds and bodies. The first steps in bringing an end to stress and tension are learning to listen to our minds and bodies, to become intimately familiar with their life and the changes they undergo. We learn to be alert to the moments in our day when our bodies begin to tense and tighten, when our minds begin to react and resist and we learn how to soften and calm in the midst of those moments.

The fundamental unity of body and mind that has always been recognized in meditative systems is increasingly being acknowledged in medicine and science. Health is no longer considered just to be a bodily state or characteristic but a state that includes both mind and body.

Emotional pain is as much a source of suffering and stress as illness and debilitation. If we reflect upon a situation in our lives when we have been gripped by anger, furious at another person or event we have found ourselves in, we easily see the way that anger fuels endless thinking, resentment and reaction. Physically we leave the situation or person yet we carry with us the endless residues of that encounter in the forms of remorse, resentment and stress in both our minds and bodies. The churning of our minds is unmistakable but the ways in which that anger is affecting our bodies are perhaps less obvious. The 'fight or flight' mechanism is stimulated within our bodies through anger and fear. As our bodies tighten and tense a series of physiological events is triggered that lead directly to stress and unease. Mindful attention given to what is actually occurring in our bodies in times of emotional pain can help us to cut through the turmoil of our thoughts, hurt feelings and confusion rather than being swept away by them. Rather than getting lost in the storms of our resentment and fear we can learn to find a place of calmness and acceptance through connecting with what is actually happening within us rather than being entangled in all of our ideas of how things 'should' be. We can learn to cultivate a simple and clear focus of attention within our bodies that becomes a foundation for calmness within our thoughts and feelings.

Reflect on a time of great happiness in your life – a time when you felt deeply connected with nature or another person. The mind softens and opens, thoughts are calm and loving, there is a heightened quality of awareness. What is happening within our bodies? There is relaxing and calming, a clear sense of ease and well-being. What happens when our bodies are ill or in pain? Thoughts and feelings of fear, anxiety, dread or depression frequently follow, which in turn influence our relationship to our bodies and the very way in which we experience pain itself, often magnifying and intensifying its impact.

In the absence of mindfulness and inner listening many of our reactions become habitual and mechanical and stress and tension find a home in our bodies. Patterns of stress such as anxiety or self-consciousness become locked into our postures and our muscles, often manifesting as chronic pain and illness. In more extreme cases this effect upon our bodies escalates into ulcers, headaches, back pain, high blood pressure, insomnia and the whole range of illnesses that are a product of stressful living. The habitual nature of our reactions and ways of storing stress can be undone through attention and mindfulness. We can learn to listen with great care and sensitivity to our bodies, our minds, our behaviour and the ways in which we interact with the world. By coming to know our bodies and minds intimately through attention and sensitivity we

99

can learn new pathways of calmness, peace, harmony, integration and respect. We may not be able to control the world but all of us have the capacity for mindfulness and sensitivity.

An important ingredient in learning to step out of the spiral of stress is the willingness to acknowledge that stress may not be intrinsic in all of the events, demands or challenges we encounter, but primarily lies in the ways in which we respond to and receive those demands and challenges. To be faced with a deadline is for one person overwhelming, for another inspiring. The prospect of moving house leads one person to feelings of panic and another to feelings of excitement. Making a presentation to a large group of people may be greeted with terror or with a sense of challenge. The events that evoke feelings of helplessness in one person, evoke excitement and eagerness in another.

We can bring our own habitual patterns and habits of fear and resistance into the variety of situations we encounter in our lives. The power of our reactions, the feelings of being out of control, helpless or powerless that accompany those reactions are powerful sources of stress. Through meditation we can learn to relieve the symptoms of stress by cultivating calmness and attention. We can also learn the skills that allow us more deeply to explore our habitual fears and develop the understanding that allows us to uproot the tendencies of mind that are the source of tension and resistance. Our life serves as our teacher in this exploration, inviting us to bring mindfulness rather than disconnection into all of those events and situations that provoke resistance and anxiety. Rather than being lost in fear we become, through mindfulness, deeply interested in the situations, events and encounters where we find ourselves most prone to anxiety and confusion. We can learn to be increasingly present in those moments – instead of fleeing from ourselves or surrendering to helplessness, we can learn to bring attention to our inner experience and find a foundation of calmness and alertness. We can learn to connect with the life of our bodies, minds and emotions in those moments and to befriend the processes that are taking place. In doing this we forsake the role of the helpless victim and become a conscious participant in understanding what is actually happening in that moment. It is a significant and transformative shift that opens a whole range of new possibilities. Rather than events, emotions and reactions happening 'to' us, we forge a relationship of calm exploration. Rather than being swept away by circumstances seemingly out of our control, we are established in one moment at a time with a mindful presence. The power is taken out of our reactions and anxieties, there is attention rather than habit, understanding rather than mindless or blind reaction.

The great gift of mindful attention is its mobility. You don't need to sit in formal meditation, close your eyes or cut off from the world in order to be aware. It can be fostered in any moment, any circumstance and any activity. It is something to experiment with for yourself. In any situation or moment when you find yourself beginning to tighten, react or tense, discover what happens if in that moment you bring your attention directly into your body to acknowledge the variety of sensations and processes that are occurring. Take just a few moments to connect with your breathing or to give careful attention to the thoughts or emotions that are present. Attention enables us to slow down the process of reaction and tension, as we connect clearly with what is actually taking place in our inner reality. Slowing down offers choices – there is the possibility of calmness, ease and clarity. There is through this non-judgmental attentiveness the beginning of acceptance and understanding. Learning to calm down our minds and bodies and to listen inwardly are the first steps in reducing stress and cultivating well-being. There may be much we need to learn about our inner world of expectations, wants, fears and ambitions that lead to stress and tension and attention is the primary foundation for this learning.

You do not need to be an expert in meditation or have a long history of spiritual experience in order to be mindful. We can all do it. When we get lost or swept away by circumstances or thoughts we can all begin again to bring mindfulness to the very next moment. The more we become familiar with being attentive and present, the easier it becomes. As our familiarity with mindfulness deepens we find that our attention is increasingly present in the beginnings of the movements of resistance, anxiety and tension. Our skill in letting go, relaxing and cultivating calmness grows.

As the demand for our time and attention grows in our lives there needs to be an equal escalation of the time we reserve for cultivating calmness and mindfulness. These times dedicated to connecting with attentiveness, quietness and well-being are not luxuries but a necessity if we value health, peace and understanding. The objection is at times raised that if we are too calm or mindful we will lose the skills we need to meet the demands and busyness of our lives. The truth is that we are most creative, organized and productive when we are calmly established in mindfulness. The skills of attention and sensitivity can be fostered anywhere, yet their development rests upon our own willingness to deeply value peace, serenity and understanding.

Being Where We Are

Reducing stress and fostering calmness rely not just upon taking time out to meditate but equally on learning to be more aware and sensitive at times when we are likely to become lost in mental activities, in busyness or preoccupation – this is when we build up stress and sacrifice mindfulness and connectedness. It is clear that we need to give as much attention to the quality of our lives as we do to what we accomplish and produce. Well-being, health and peace demand a change in attitude and approach to many of the activities we engage in through our days. The guiding principle of awareness is concerned with 'being where we are' rather than with arriving somewhere else; giving attention to the quality of 'how' we act, speak, work and live rather than just to the goals we are intent on. It is a practice of the present moment, bringing calm and sensitive attention to every moment, every task and every inter-action. This primary principle is what enables the deepening of meditation; equally, it can be applied to every moment of our day to enable us to live calmly rather than stressfully.

Instead of fuming with impatience as we wait for a bus or sit in a traffic jam we can bring mindfulness into our bodies or into listen-ing and cultivate calmness. Instead of approaching any task, whether it is washing dishes or a work assignment, intent on the moment it will be completed, we can bring a calm attention to be present in each movement involved in the task. Instead of convers-ing with another person impatient to prove our point or assert an opinion we can bring a sensitive attention to listening wholeheart-edly. Intent only on destinations, completions and ending we are disconnected from where we are – we are ignoring our minds and bodies and in doing so creating a primary source of stress. You do not need a special moment or posture to be aware – with conscious attention your life becomes your meditation room.

Beginnings and Endings

One of the primary sources of stress is the way in which we accumulate and carry excess and unnecessary thoughts through our day. Many times we have to leave conversations, activities and tasks incomplete and turn our attention to another activity that demands our immediate attention. Through inattention we carry, through thought, these moments of incompletion and unfinished business, creating a background feeling of anxiety and pressure within our minds and bodies. Our attention becomes divided as we attempt to both carry our thoughts about the encounter we have left and attend to the present. We find ourselves unable to be wholeheartedly present in the moment as our attention is still entangled with the moment that has already gone. It is an ineffective use of thought; this divided attention leads to non-productive anxiety, as we worry about both past and future. It is this background pressure within the mind and body that leads us to become overly reactive to even small demands and feelings of stress in the face of escalating demands. There is a rare skilfulness involved in learning to be present, to let go of what is not actually requiring our attention in the moment and to attend fully to what is requiring our attention. Being fully present in one moment at a time we discover an emerging calmness in both mind and body.

Simplicity and calmness in our day, our life, can be cultivated through paying close attention to the numerous beginnings and endings that are part of our day and to learn to pause for a moment in that gap between the ending of one interaction and the beginning of the next. A conversation ends and before we turn our attention to the next engagement we can take a moment to remind ourselves to be fully present in a single breath. A task is completed so, before throwing ourselves into the next, we can take a moment to be fully present within our bodies, aware of our posture or our feet touching the ground. These small gaps between ending one task and beginning the next can become precious moments of calm and mindfulness – times to take a moment to be still and check in with the quality of our mind and body.

Mindfulness With the Sense Doors

A skilful relationship to our sense doors and all of the endless information that presents itself to our eyes, ears, nose and body is a direct way of cultivating calmness of being. Instead of overloading our sense doors and therefore overloading our minds, we can seek simplicity and wholehearted attentiveness. Walking down a busy street we are assailed by countless sights and sounds that seem to demand our attention. Without mindfulness our attention is captured by this barrage of impressions and our thoughts about them. There is another way of taking that same walk. We can walk down the same street holding within our attention a primary focus, that excludes nothing yet that is steadily established in just one sense door. We can give attention to walking and all of the subtle movements of our body involved in taking a single step. We can give primary attention to what is right before us, bringing sensitivity and connectedness. If we listen to music we can give our attention to listening wholeheartedly; reading a book with care and mindfulness becomes a training in sensitivity and awareness. Attention brought wholeheartedly to one moment at a time is the key principle in cultivating calmness and well-being of body and mind and dissolving stress and tension. As we learn to bring wholehearted attention to the ordinary activities of our day – eating, speaking, playing and listening – they are transformed into moments of sensitivity and calm.

Times for Stillness

To begin and end our day with a dedicated period of stillness and attention is of inestimable value in approaching our day with calmness and ending our day with a sense of completion and mindfulness. Even fifteen minutes given to meditation when we get up in the morning and before we go to sleep has a profound impact upon the quality of our mind and body – giving us the opportunity to relax and be calm. We are training ourselves in calmness rather than deepening our patterns of tension and holding. A number of the styles of meditation previously discussed can be utilized during these times. Several of them, such as learning to focus our attention upon our breathing not only in formal meditation periods, but also at frequent times throughout the day, help us to pause and collect our attention and are particularly effective in decreasing stress and tension. The following meditations are specific meditation practices that calm the mind and body, and can be developed in our lives.

Mindfulness of the Body

To cultivate well-being and learn the skill of body calmness we need to be intimately acquainted with our bodies, experiencing them directly. A powerful and direct way of seeing directly the changes our bodies go through and cultivating calmness is through adapting the style of body-scanning meditation previously discussed under mindfulness practices. Lying down on your back the attention is systematically moved through every area of your body. There is no attempt to make anything special happen, yet in this movement of attention through your body there is a natural integration of body and mind and a fostering of well-being.

Lying on your back, begin by bringing your attention to the top of your head, simply noticing any sensations that are present. From this point expand your attention to include all of your head, face and neck. Continue this downward movement of your body through each arm and hand, then return to your head again. Move the attention down through the trunk of your body and then through each leg. Move the attention slowly, simply feeling what is happening in each part of your body as your attention touches it. You may notice a change from superficially experiencing the surface of your body to feeling that you are deeply within your body. As the mind is steadily focused in the body there is a releasing of body tensions and frequently a simultaneous releasing of all of the thoughts and images previously dominating the mind. In the movement of attention through your body pay particular attention to those areas which are prone to accumulating tension such as your face, shoulders, neck and stomach. Let your attention rest for some moments in these areas, exploring them, breathing into them and consciously relaxing. Once you have completed a full scan of the body, lie for a time with an awareness that includes the whole of your body. If you feel a return of tightening or tension bring your attention to focus very fully upon that area. Cultivating the body awareness is cultivating a present moment awareness that calms not only the body but also the mind.

Chronic Pain

Increasingly meditation is being recognized as an effective tool for understanding and alleviating chronic pain conditions. Chronic pain differs immensely from acute pain which has a recognizable cause and often a solution. Acute pain happens when we stub our toe, have a dose of flu or break an elbow. It is time-limited pain – it can be cured and it will end. The nature of chronic pain is that it does not always have a recognizable cause and its end is unknown.

Chronic pain has become part of life for increasing numbers of people. It is an area of stress that requires a radical shift in attitude and approach; this is where meditation is particularly effective. All pain evokes in us the initial desire to get rid of it, make it go away or find a formula to cure it. When we become entrenched in these desires our pain becomes suffering; we become victims and are caught in increasingly deep feelings of powerlessness and despair. The calmness and understanding we can find through bringing a meditative approach to chronic pain can drastically reduce the levels of suffering that become associated with it.

Through meditation practice we learn to approach our pain directly, to open to it and to explore it in a detailed way. In doing this there is a letting go of the desire to get rid of it and we cease to relate to pain as an opponent. We learn to establish ourselves in calmness and acceptance. We learn to let go of the judgements, fear and resistance which have the effect of intensifying pain and further alienating us from our bodies. It is a profound shift in attitude that does not guarantee to cure chronic pain, yet numerous studies have shown that it alleviates the impact of pain and enables those with chronic pain to find a quality of life that is not wholly defined by pain.

Through practices such as mindfulness with breathing and body-scanning the solidity of painful areas of the body is broken down as they are explored in detail with a calm attentiveness. Pain is a tapestry of sensations that ebb and flow, with points of intensity which undergo change on a moment-to-moment level. Penetrating the solidity of areas of pain there emerges a relationship of interest and acceptance. Using meditation to alleviate pain requires immense patience and commitment. There will be days when it is deeply effective, other days when it appears to make little difference. Consistently and patiently bringing a meditative approach to chronic

pain will transform our relationship to it – it becomes our teacher
and the place in our lives where we learn the deepest lessons about
acceptance, openness and balance.

Our backs are an area of the body most frequently subject to chronic pain and tension. Lie down on your back in a comfortable posture. After taking a few deep breaths, bring your attention directly
to the area of your back where there is pain. First with your atttten-
tion trace its outlines. Know the areas where it begins to fade or
end. Bring your attention gently into the area that is painful. Notice
if there are points of particular intensity and gently explore them
with your attention. Notice the way the sensations change, intensifying and fading. Stay present as long as you can with a gentle,
interested attention. If the sensations feel overwhelming move your
attention into a calmer place in your body for a time, such as your
hands or your breathing. As you relax bring your attention again to
your back. Approach these sensitive areas without forcing or even
any feeling that the pain should change or disappear. Cultivate a
calm and sensitive interest.

Mindfulness with Breathing

Our breath is a constant companion and a great ally in cultivating
calmness and balance through our day. In any moment it is a focus
we can reconnect with to restore steadiness and attention. No matter where we are or what we are doing we can always take a
moment to pause and breathe with mindfulness. Learning to check
in with our breath at regular intervals during the day is a direct way
of checking in with the quality and state of our mind and body. It
returns us to the present moment providing the opportunity to let
go of tension and stress patterns.

Anxiety and tension affect our breathing as our chests tighten and constrict, which further affects the well-being of our bodies. In using mindfulness of breathing as a means of easing tension and constriction, first find a posture that provides the most calmness and relaxation in your body. It is often helpful to lie down and even place your hand on your abdomen or chest to reinforce your connection with your breathing. Initially, just notice how your breath moves in your body without forcing it in any way. Whether your breath is shallow or deep, simply pay attention to its movement and the way your body responds to it, with expansion and contraction in your abdomen or chest. Then consciously take a few deep breaths so the movement of your breath reaches into your abdomen. Again relax and let your breathing find its own natural rhythm. We are not forcing in this practice, simply exploring each breath as it occurs. As your mind and body relax your breath will become both slower and deeper. If you find that your attention again becomes entangled in thoughts, images, memories or plans, take a few fuller breaths to establish your attention once more in your body. Persevering with this practice is a direct and simple way of letting go of knots of tension that have accumulated in your body and mind.

Cultivating Well-Being

Using meditation to cultivate well-being and to alleviate stress needs to be a multi-faceted approach that includes both our inner and outer worlds. Fostering and valuing calmness may well involve changing some of our attitudes and looking at the forces of ambition, competitiveness and expectation that we bring to our lives and relationships. It may also involve carefully examining the ways in which we approach our lives. We may have unrealistic expectations about how much we should achieve in a single day, creating a stressed body and an overburdened mind. We may need to learn how to slow down in our lives, to find more moments of stillness and inner listening. Our bodies are messengers to us – they deliver clear signals when we are engaged in activities or thoughts that are not conducive to calmness and health and we need to listen carefully to them.

'Not enough time' has become the mantra of our culture and the price of well-being, sensitivity and calmness may involve being clearly realistic about what it is possible for us to address in any moment. We can slow down the momentum of intensity, yet busyness is brought to our life through habit and through being too closely identified with goals rather than with the quality of our life. We can make the time of preparing to go into our day a time of mindfulness and sensitivity that is brought to the simple tasks of dressing, showering and eating. We can take moments throughout the day to monitor what is happening in our bodies, giving attention to our shoulders, face and posture, aware of where we are storing tension and where we can relax. We can work with cultivating wholehearted attentiveness – when we are engaged with another person listening fully and making eye contact. We can use the breaks we have in the day as times of simplicity and calmness – walking, breathing, listening. We can give attention to the many transitions in our day as we move from one task to the next, taking a moment to breathe. We can stop rushing, slow down the momentum of our bodies and walk mindfully. There are many doorways to calm in each of our days and if we value health and well-being we need to discover them. As long as we are awake we can find the moments to be mindful and they are a gift to ourselves.

Doorways to Calm

1 *Choose one activity that is a regular feature of your day, such as climbing stairs or talking on the telephone. Intentionally approach this activity with calm and mindfulness.*

2 *Learn to pause and breathe mindfully at the end of each task before beginning another.*

3 *Remember to check in with your body at regular intervals during the day, paying particular attention to your shoulders, face and hands. Learn to relax.*

4 *Take the time to eat slowly and mindfully.*

5 *Be aware of those moments when your attention becomes fragmented – listening to music while reading, talking to someone while planning your next task. Explore what wholehearted attention means.*

6 *Find moments in which you can be still.*

MEDITATION
in Daily Life

Most people who undertake a meditative path will not be seeking to undertake a life as a hermit or intend to withdraw to a monastery. Our meditation will take place in the midst of our daily lives with the great variety of challenges they bring to us. Meditation would be of limited value if it were restricted to experiences achieved in formal sessions on a cushion. To achieve only brief glimpses of calmness and happiness that are forgotten or lost the moment we rise from our cushion has never been the intent of any meditative tradition. Meditation is intended to bring transformation to the whole of our lives, fostering calmness, well-being and balance in every moment and circumstance. In our formal sessions of meditation we plant the seeds of understanding, attentiveness and balance; our challenge is to further cultivate those seeds in the midst of all the changing activities and interactions of our life.

Some of the most important moments in our meditative journey take place not when seated with our eyes closed, but in those moments when we leave the cushion and enter into our life. These are the moments that invite us to learn what it means to live in a meditative spirit, approaching our life with an openness and commitment to deepen in sensitivity, mindfulness and understanding. These are the times when we are asked to find calm within chaos, peace in the midst of conflict and clarity when surrounded by confusion. The lessons we learn in the structures of our formal meditation come to life only when they are applied to transform the daily encounters and activities of our lives.

Awareness is more than an exercise, it is a journey of a lifetime. Meditation is not a passive state, neither does it isolate us in an ivory tower from where we can view the unfolding events of our world and life with a benign detachment or disinterest. It is not intended to bring about a state of disconnection where we feel indifferent or invulnerable to the world around us, but is intended to magnify connectedness and teach us the way to be a conscious participant in every moment. Travelling a meditative path is learning the skill of making calmness, clarity and understanding part of our everyday life, where nothing is exempt from a caring attentiveness.

There is a profound happiness and richness that is born of meditative experience and understanding, yet the intention in practice of meditation is not dedicated to achieving only pleasant states of experience or blissful pinnacles. Meditation would be of minimal value if it could be cultivated only in the midst of pleasant experiences, good health, supportive circumstances, when surrounded by caring people. Our life is comprised of many pleasant moments and interactions that delight and enrich us and meditation teaches us to appreciate them deeply. Equally in our lives we encounter moments and interactions that distress and challenge us – times of ill-health, encounters with hostility, pressure and confrontation. We all meet praise and blame, success and failure, loss and separation and the variety of responses that can arise within ourselves in relationship to these experiences. As these moments are part of the reality of our lives and world, they must equally be part of our meditation. Rather than fleeing from or avoiding these moments or greeting them with the extremes of disappointment, distress or even fragile exhilaration, meditation can teach us to approach them clearly and directly, to find balance and understanding in the midst of all events. Unpredictability, times of confusion, disorder and circumstances that we cannot control will feature in all of our lives. Resistance, avoidance and fear lead only to anxiety and disconnection. Learning to live in a meditative spirit means cultivating the willingness to approach the unpleasant and difficult with the same commitment to attentiveness and understanding that we bring to the moments of delight and happiness.

Meditation is not a prescription or a solution to the difficulties and challenges we inevitably encounter in our lives, but will teach us the power that attentiveness has to transform the overwhelming or seemingly impossible moments we meet, into moments that can be approached with balance, calmness and understanding. These moments, if approached with a meditative spirit, become guides and teachers for us that show us the way to deepen in understanding and compassion. Through the skills we learn in meditation we begin to discern the difference between those events and moments we need to embrace with acceptance and understanding and the moments that ask for clear and conscious action, wise and honest speech and transformation. Through our meditation practice we become intimately acquainted with a refuge of inner calm and balance which is brought to the changing circumstances and moments of our lives. Meditation does not promise an 'ideal' world where we are never disturbed or challenged; it empowers us to live in the 'real' world with awareness and understanding.

Meditation is a path of transformation which, practised well, has the power to transform not only our inner reality but the whole of our lives. The calming down we experience within ourselves manifests in the calming down of our lives. The attentiveness and clarity of seeing we cultivate within ourselves becomes the foundation for clear actions, speech and choices. The care we learn to extend to the quality of our inner world is extended to all of our relationships so that they mirror the honesty, calmness and understanding we value inwardly. Formal meditation is primarily concerned with inner development but the true spirit of meditation is one that equally embraces our inner and outer world. Meditation comes alive only when it is embodied in the whole of our lives.

A meditative spirit essentially means that we approach our lives with an attitude that every moment is significant, an invitation to cultivate understanding, sensitivity and attentiveness. There is nothing that is considered 'worldly', 'mundane' or unworthy of our attentiveness. We learn to approach all experiences – doing the laundry, washing the dishes, working, playing and formal meditation as opportunities to find harmony and understanding. To deepen in meditation we must learn to end the dichotomy of a spiritual life and a worldly life. This division will bring endless frustration if our meditation is seen to happen in only brief, reserved moments – separate from the rest of our lives and so doing little to transform them. Awareness is not an activity or solely a practice; it is a way of seeing directly, immediately and with great sensitivity into each moment.

The principle of establishing and cultivating attentiveness is the primary principle developed in all styles of formal meditation disciplines. It is equally the foundation that enables our meditation practice to extend in a way in which it touches and transforms the whole of our lives. Cultivating a balanced and calm attentiveness in our lives requires the same effort and clear intention that is required in formal meditation practice. Superficially it appears easier not to be wholeheartedly attentive in our lives but to live instead habitually, with a mind that endlessly churns out thoughts, avoiding difficult situations and striving to maintain pleasant situations. Yet the results of these familiar patterns are inner pressure, disconnection and discontent. Effort is needed for us to learn new ways of being in ourselves and in the world.

The results of cultivating the effort and intention to be attentive in our lives are immediate and enriching. There is an enhanced sensitivity in our seeing, listening, actions and speech. Attuned to the

117

movements of our minds and emotions in relationship to the world we become less judgmental and increasingly open and receptive. There is a greater ease and calmness in our minds and bodies and our thoughts, decisions and speech become simpler and more effective. Our access to a deeper intuitive way of perceiving is enhanced as we forge more direct and immediate connections with each moment and each interaction. Through cultivating attentiveness we find ourselves more fully present in one moment at a time and our preoccupations with past and future lessen in intensity.

The dimension of cultivating attentiveness in all circumstances, moments and interactions is a primary ingredient in furthering the process of discovery and transformation. We all have the capacity to be attentive and present, it is a capacity that is deepened and strengthened through our practice and application. In formal meditation times attention is directly cultivated; in informal times in our lives there are a variety of clues and exercises that help us to sustain and deepen our capacity for awareness and sensitivity. The effectiveness of these exercises rests upon the willingness and interest we bring to their application and exploration.

The cultivation of meditation in an inclusive and holistic way involves bringing a meditative spirit and clear attentiveness to the different dimensions of our experience that are not separate but interconnected. We learn to be directly and deeply attentive to the quality of our inner world – our bodies, emotions and mind. Equally we learn to bring the skills and principles fundamental to our meditation practice to the relationships we have with other people and events. Learning to bring an attitude of care and sensitivity to even the small tasks and interactions of our day we nourish our own practice and embody care and awareness in each moment of our day.

Formal Meditation Practice

A daily meditation practice requires both discipline and effort yet it is the cornerstone of integrating meditation into the rest of our lives. Times of formal meditation, even if they are only brief periods of fifteen minutes or half an hour, need to become a priority in our lives. Our practice is kept alive by reserving times in our day that are dedicated to calmness and stillness. To have a regular time and place that is committed to formal meditation is often the most effective way of sustaining a regular practice. The styles or techniques explored in these times are of secondary importance. The different styles previously mentioned which highlight the different principles of meditation, such as concentration, devotion, mindfulness and relaxation, can be utilized according to our own temporament and what actually works for us. What is of primary importance is that we have a time that is dedicated to coming back to ourselves and the present moment; a time of reconnection and calmness. In the midst of a busy life, clear intention is of great importance as we approach our times of formal meditation. They are not times for planning the activities of the next day or rehashing all the interactions and activities that we have encountered in the day we have just completed. The value of the times of formal meditation ripens through our intention to use these times fully to be aware of one moment at a time, to cultivate calmness and clarity of being, attentiveness and sensitivity.

Daily meditation practice requires tremendous patience. We may experience our minds as being overfull, bursting with thought, our bodies may be tired, we may see the repetitive recycling of the residues of our day. All of these activities do not mean that our meditation is worthless, neither should they be treated as obstacles to negate. In the midst of all of this we foster some of the deepest principles and lessons of meditation – patience, acceptance, balance, simplicity and dedication. Wise and kind attention is to see and let go, to allow the swirl of thoughts and feelings to arise and to pass.

If you have only a short time available for formal meditation it is often helpful to develop a simple practice such as focusing upon the breath or your body as a way of establishing yourself in the present moment, in sensitivity and attentiveness. Every moment of doing this is worthwhile, affects the quality of our mind and body and is an essential factor in enabling our awareness and understanding to mature. Be careful not to look for signs of progress and improvement. There will be meditation periods of great calmness, concentration and insight. There may be other periods where we feel overwhelmed by endless thoughts and feelings. The way in which understanding and attention matures is both unpredictable and somewhat mysterious. We may be tempted into thinking our meditation is unproductive or a waste of time, and yet when we get up off our cushion we find to our surprise that we are approaching our day with a tangible sense of attentiveness and clarity.

More prolonged periods of formal meditation in retreats or courses where there is both guidance and community are of inestimable value in deepening practice and self-confidence. There are a variety of organizations dedicated to supporting people in their practice through offering a range of retreats and courses dedicated to meditation (see Resource Guide). Even if these do not interest us or if we do not have the time available, it may be possible at times to take an afternoon or a day that we reserve entirely for exploring our meditation practice. They can be times when we turn off the telephone and create a meditative space around us. Spending such periods of time alone, developing calmness and stillness, exploring our meditation practice can make a significant impact upon the rest of our week.

Walking

Walking is an integral part of our day as we move from one room to another, one engagement to the next, as we travel to and from work. This simple activity can be performed habitually or can become an exercise in mindfulness. We can experiment with designating these times of walking as times that we reconnect with our bodies and through this, with the present moment. Give attention to all the subtle shifts that are involved in taking a single step, in the sensation of your foot touching the ground. Through giving attention to our bodies in walking we integrate the mind and the body and establish attentiveness. This very ordinary activity that is part of all of our days is transformed through attentiveness, becoming a time of sensitivity and wakefulness. We can experiment with being aware of the moments when our walking is rushed or harried, how our bodies are expressing a state of mind in that moment that is not conducive to calmness and ease. As we walk in our day, we can be walking our meditative path, not primarily focused on reaching our destination but experiencing a time of mindfulness and being present in the moment.

Mindful Eating

Meditation practice is a process of deepening in sensitivity in the very ordinary activities of our life. Each day we give time to nourishing our body, to preparing food and eating. These times can be moments of habit and distractedness or equally times of deep

121

sensitivity and awareness. We can adopt the discipline of mindful eating – ensuring that we always sit down to eat, that we approach this time calmly and slowly and with the intention to be fully present. Take a moment to savour and finish a single mouthful of food before you lift your fork to take the next. Bring mindful attention to the taste and sensations of each piece of food you eat. Be aware of your posture as you eat, ensuring that your body is relaxed and at ease. Experiment with reserving one meal in the day to eat in silence. As we bring attention to these times the ordinary events in our lives are transformed – body, mind and the present moment are unified through our attentiveness. We are consciously cultivating well-being and harmony in those moments; qualities that become increasingly natural and instinctive to us as we experiment and practice.

Simplicity

Consciously cultivating simplicity in our lives and within ourselves is one of the most direct means of achieving well-being, peace and harmony. It is one of the primary principles of meditation that when carried into the way we live our lives directly deepens understanding. Simplicity does not require that we resign our jobs or give all of our possessions to charity. In formal meditation we cultivate simplicity through attending to our minds, bodies and motions without judgement, evaluation or comparison. We learn to be with the moment-to-moment changes occurring within us just as they are without adding or subtracting anything. This simplicity we cultivate in formal meditation can be directly applied to our life. We learn to be aware of those times in interaction with the world around us when we are adding excess layers of judgement or evaluation and thus subtracting from our capacity to be wholeheartedly present.

Bringing a wholehearted attention to our conversations and activities is directly cultivating simplicity. Are we listening well? Are our actions undertaken with mindfulness? Instead of thinking about the moment or trying to leap into the next moment with our thoughts, we directly experience where we are. Instead of being lost in all of our ideas of how things should be, we are directly connected with how things actually are. This simplicity calms the mind and body, fostering harmony and well-being.

Simplicity is equally cultivated through giving attention to our lifestyles. Excessive complexity, entanglement and busyness in our lifestyles will create a corresponding complexity, entanglement and busyness within our consciousness. If we deeply value a calmer, more open and sensitive mind and heart it may involve some simplification of our lives. Cultivating simplicity has profound implications not only for the quality of our own well-being, but equally for the quality of our world. In voluntary or conscious simplicity as a way of life we are taking only that which we need. We are learning to let go of the greed and wanting which does not in reality enrich our lives but only creates entanglement. Living in a way of conscious simplicity we create the possibility for a deeper compassion and sense of interconnectedness to emerge from within ourselves. Simplicity and sensitivity are closely related. Our meditation practice, through simplicity, becomes a visible way of honouring and respecting ourselves, other people, our environment and the world we share.

Spiritual Community

Many people find themselves quite contented with following a meditative path alone. For others, taking time to meet with other people who share similar aspirations and direction can be deeply nourishing. It can provide an opportunity to discuss difficulties that are encountered and alleviate the sense of loneliness that can arise when practising alone. We discover that we are not unique in struggling with many of the obstacles we meet, we receive encouragement and support from others. Community is an intrinsic part of most spiritual traditions that offers an affirmation of our quest and path. In the western world community does not imply leaving our homes and moving into a collective, nor does it imply fundamentalism, sectarianism or separation. Community happens whenever like-minded people meet together in a spirit of openness and honesty, dedicating time for reflection, communication and meditation.

A Practice of Integrity

In exploring the different traditions of meditation it is evident that there is a shared agreement that an ethical life provides the foundation for depth in meditation and for a mind that is easily collected in calmness and happiness. Ethics are not just rules or ways of defining right and wrong, good and bad. Ethics can be adopted as a practice that is a powerful way to awaken sensitivity and awareness in our lives. Ethics concern the quality of our actions, speech and thoughts and serve as a basis for reflection and not as a basis for judgement or punishment. Ethics provides guidelines for cultivating inner and outer relationships of integrity, compassion, tolerance and forgiveness.

We can adopt sensitivity in our relationships as a practice we bring directly into our lives. Speech is our primary vehicle of communication, that connects us with others and through which we express ourselves. Our words make a powerful impression upon others.

They have the potential to be a vehicle for hurting or alienating others; they equally have the potential to be a vehicle that expresses acceptance and sensitivity. Giving attention to our speech reveals those moments when our words are motivated by habit, anger, intolerance or harshness. The same attention also offers us the possibility of travelling new pathways in our lives, allowing our speech to be a means of expressing sensitivity, compassion and understanding. As a practice we can establish the intention to simply bring greater mindfulness to those moments in our day when we are in contact with others, to be aware of the words we are using and what is being expressed. Learning the art of listening inwardly we become increasingly skilled in bringing wholehearted attention to listening to others.

In the same way through our actions, choices and thoughts we affect the world around us and the quality of our own minds and hearts. The great power of attention is that it dissolves habit. Rather than being governed by impulsive reactions or entangled feelings, we can, through developing attention, be guided by compassion, understanding and sensitivity. The basic principle that informs a life of sensitivity and integrity is the essential reflection upon what leads to conflict, harm and sorrow and what it is that leads to peace, well-being and understanding. This primary reflection can be related to our actions, speech, thoughts and choices, showing us the path to a life of integrity and a mind and heart of calmness, awareness and compassion.

Dissolving Habit

A powerful method for integrating awareness and sensitivity into the activities of our daily lives is to focus attention upon areas where you find yourself consistently habitual. Simply select one area of your life that you give little attention to because of familiarity – the way you eat or dress, the time you travel to and from work, the way you walk or sit, the way you speak to your partner or a family member. Establish the clear intention to approach that activity as if you had never encountered it before. Give careful attention to how you use your body, the movements of your hands, the way you listen or your speech. This is not an attempt to find the 'right' way to engage in any of these activities. It is an exploration to discover the way in which the simple, ordinary activities of our lives are transformed by attentiveness. Through attention we learn the skill of being whole-heartedly present with great sensitivity. Every moment of dissolving habit with clear attentiveness is a moment of fostering sensitivity and a clear connection with the present moment. It is learning to see all things, all people and ourselves anew, free from the filter of images, conclusions or assumptions. Our capacity to see, listen and act with freshness is a primary foundation for deepening in understanding.

Reflection Upon Difficult Circumstances

Meditation is not intended to shelter us from the moments of conflict and difficulty we meet in our lives but to provide us with the inner resources and skills to approach them with greater understanding and calmness. There may be situations in our lives where there is repetitive tension, misunderstanding and conflict. Repetitive conflict is most often a signal to us that there is a need for greater understanding and new ways of approaching the situations we resist or fear. The possibility of discovering greater calmness, ease and understanding in these moments of tension relies upon our willingness to give attention to them.

There are different dimensions to the attention we can learn to bring to stressful situations. Before going into a situation where there has been recurring tension it is helpful to bring your attention into both your body and the feelings that are present. Be aware of how you might be tensing up or where there are already thoughts or feelings of resistance, fear or aversion. Use your attention to carefully explore these areas of holding or contraction, letting your body relax and holding the feelings in the light of an accepting, sensitive attention. When in the midst of the situation that is challenging, stay in touch with your body, consciously relaxing. There are times when it is important to reflect upon the relationship or interaction that distresses us. What would we need to let go of or to cultivate to allow this interaction to develop and change? Is there anger or fear that is rooted in the past that is preventing us from meeting the present with clarity and honesty? Do we need to find greater depths of compassion or tolerance in the present? Do we need to be more honest and clear in our own communication? Reflection serves a significant role in cultivating understanding. Reflection is different from obsessive or repetitive thinking. At times it involves the simple and clear contemplation of a single question that is held in the light of clear attention that encourages a more intuitive response to emerge from within ourselves. Clearly repetitive conflict or tension becomes the breeding ground of endless thinking and reaction. It is an area that calls for clear attention and enquiry.

Reflective Themes

It can be useful to select a particular theme of enquiry that we hold in our attention for a period of several days or a week at a time. It can be a theme such as generosity, anxiety, wholehearted listening, anger or being aware of beginnings and endings as they occur in our day. Wise speech, impermanence, resistance or compassion can all serve as themes of enquiry. It is helpful to choose a theme that is meaningful for us. It might be an area of our lives where we become repeatedly stuck or a quality we would wish to deepen in. When we awaken in the morning simply plant the intention in our conscious-ness to explore the theme as we move through the various activities of our day. Before going to sleep at night, spend a few moments reflecting upon the way in which the theme you have adopted has appeared in our day and the ways we have related to it.

Exploring a reflective theme does not involve endless contempla-tion, neither does it imply self-consciousness in our interactions. By simply planting the seed of intention which highlights a particular reflective theme, we become increasingly aware of the way it informs our lives. This kind of exploration is a direct way of inte-grating our formal meditation practice into the activities of our lives. It has the power to awaken both interest and understanding.

Inspiration

Inspiration and interest are necessary ingredients in deepening and sustaining any spiritual journey. It is obviously easy to feel both interested and inspired when our meditation experiences are rich and fruitful, when there are dramatic insights or experiences. It is far more challenging to remain interested and inspired when our meditation feels flat or dry. When we feel interested and inspired we have an abundance of energy and effort to bring to exploring our meditation practice. In periods of barrenness it is more challenging to find the energy and effort that are needed to reawaken our interest. There are valleys and peaks in all spiritual journeys and in those moments when our meditation feels stuck it is helpful to explore the ways in which we might nourish and reawaken our interest.

Meditation deepens and develops through awakening and cultivating the many factors of effort, intention, dedication and interest. The nourishment that vitalizes and gives life to our meditation is also consciously cultivated in a variety of different ways.

Mindful reading is one source of nourishment. We can read in a way in which we are intent on consuming as much information as possible, much of which we quickly forget. We can also read in a reflective way. Choosing a book that is meaningful to us and using it as a basis for contemplation. Perhaps staying with a single line or chapter that speaks to our hearts and sense of aspiration for a prolonged period of time. As we read we question the ways in which the message we are absorbing relates to our own experience.

Formal meditation, meeting with like-minded people, spending time in nature and reflection are all ways of awakening and sustaining interest in our meditative journey. Just as any plant requires the nourishment of soil, water and sun to grow, the deepening of our own meditation practice relies upon the nourishment we provide. The primary nourishment for interest and inspiration is found within our deepening experience of meditation. The direct experience of deepening levels of calmness, happiness and clarity discovered in and through our meditation practice reveals to us the possibilities for transformation and depth that lie within ourselves.

RESOURCE
Guide

For anyone wanting to explore meditation at this time there is a remarkable range of options open to them. Meditation is increasingly being absorbed into our mainstream culture – included in a variety of health care systems, prisons, schools and work settings. Meditation practice is no longer the sole territory of those leading a religious life, but has instead become an integral part of the lives of countless people who value calmness and understanding and who seek to develop a spiritual core in their lives that doesn't demand withdrawal from the world. There is a vast variety of traditions. Some of these choose to closely align their meditative teachings with a religious philosophy where other traditions have adapted enormously to meet the changing needs and attitudes of our Western lifestyles and culture.

It would not be possible, nor is it the role of this book to provide an exhaustive list of the variety of centres and schools that will offer instruction in meditation. What is included here is a brief list of centres that can be contacted for information and instruction. Mention of any centre listed does not imply endorsement, it is up to each individual to discover whether the direction given in any centre or tradition is aligned with their own temperament and aspiration. The centres listed here will not expect any particular religious affiliation nor will attempt to impose any.

Australia

Dhammananda Forest Centre, Bodhi Farm, The Channon, Via Lismore, NSW 2480. Contact for programme of retreats offered.

WAY of

Canada

Westcoast Dharma Society, 2224 Larch Street, Vancouver, BC V6K 3P7. Primarily offers weekend non-residential retreats and affiliated with a larger meditation group that offers classes and longer retreats.

France

La Borie Noble, 38650 Roqueredonde, Herault (34). An ecumenical, Gandhian Ark Community based on principles of self-sufficiency, open year round to all.

Communauté de Taize, 71250 Taize, Saone-et-Loire, telephone 85 50 18 18. An ecumenical spiritual centre open all year to people from all backgrounds.

Plum Village – Village des Pruniers, Meyrace, 47120 Loubes-Bernac, telephone 33(0)16 53 96 75 40. A Zen-Vietnamese centre under the guidance of Thich Nhat Hanh. Various retreats and opportunities to participate in the life of the resident community are available through the year.

Germany

Buddha-Haus Stadtzentrum, Klarastrasse 4, 80636 Munchen, telephone +49(0)89 1238868. A Theravada centre that offers a range of opportunities to learn meditation in weekend, day-long and longer seminars.

Haus der Stille, Muhlenweg 20, D-21514 Roseburg über Buchen, telephone 04158 214. Offers a wide range of residential retreats drawing on all traditions of Buddhism. Comprehensive meditation instruction offered.

Seminarhaus Engl, Engl 1, 84339 Unterdietfurt, telephone +49(0)8728 616. A retreat environment offering a varied programme that draws upon all traditions.

Zentrum für Buddhismus, Waldhaus am Lachersee, D-56643 Nickenish. A comprehensive range of non-sectarian residential retreats offered through the year. Write for programme.

Italy

AMECO, Via Valle di Riva 1, 00141 Roma. Organizes a wide range of classes and retreats in Rome and elsewhere in Italy. Write for information.

The Netherlands

European Buddhist Union's European Buddhist Directory, EBU c/o BUN, PO Box 17286, 1001 JG Amsterdam. For comprehensive listing of centres and meditation teaching throughout Europe.

Vipassana Meditation Foundation (Theravada), Kamerlingh Onnesstraat 71, 9727 HG Groningen, telephone +31(0)50 5276051. Offers retreats and classes with meditation instruction based on the Theravada tradition of Buddhism.

New Zealand

Te Moata Meditation Centre, PO Box 100, Tairu, telephone 64 7868 8798.

South Africa

Buddhist Retreat Centre, PO Box 131, Ixopo 4630, telephone 0336 341863. Offers a range of retreats and instructions in meditation in a year-round programme.

Switzerland

Dhamma Gruppe, Postfach 5909, CH 3001, Bern. Co-ordinates an ongoing retreat programme in Switzerland and throughout Europe led by a variety of different teachers. Write for schedule.

United Kingdom

Amaravati Buddhist Monastery, Great Gaddesden, Hemel Hempstead, Hertfordshire HP1 3BZ, telephone 01442 843239. A Theravada Buddhist centre which offers instruction and guidance to both beginning and experienced meditators under the guidance of resident monks and nuns. Has several affiliated monasteries and centres in England and around the world.

The Buddhist Society, 58 Eccleston Square, London SW1V 1PH, telephone 020 7834 5858. Aims for impartial presentation of main Buddhist tradition in the form of classes and activities. Offers an extensive library and provides information about the variety of Buddhist centres in England.

Gaia House, West Ogwell, Newton Abbot, Devon TQ12 6EN, telephone 01626 333613. Gaia House is a registered charity offering a wide range of residential retreats varying in length from a weekend to a month that are open to people from all backgrounds and are suitable for beginning and experienced meditators. The meditation instruction draws from all the main Buddhist traditions without the imposition of any religious belief. Also offers day-long meditation retreats in London and has a wide network of meditation groups. Call or write for retreat programme.

The National Retreat Centre, 24 South Audley Street, London S1Y 5DL, telephone 020 7493 3534. This is an ecumenical resource centre which provides information on Christian retreat houses and programmes around the country.

Ramakrishna Order, Unity House, Blind Lane, Bourne End, Buckinghamshire SL8 5LG, telephone 01626 26464. A Hindu Interfaith temple that welcomes people from all faiths for private and group retreats.

Throssel Hole Priory, Carrshield, Hexham, Northumberland NE47 8AL, telephone 01434 345204. A Soto Zen meditation centre offering a range of retreats and meditation instruction. There are a large number of affiliated groups around the world. Introductory courses for beginners.

United States

Insight Meditation Society, 1230 Pleasant Street, Barre, Mass 01005, telephone 617 355 4378. Offers a year-round programme of meditation retreats open to people from all backgrounds and suitable for beginning and experienced meditators.

WAY of

Spirit Rock, 5000 Sir Francis Drake Boulevard, PO Box 909, Woodacre, CA 94973, telephone 415 488 0164. Offers both a widely-varied community and a retreat programme primarily based in the Buddhist tradition but open to people of all backgrounds and ages.

Dr Jon Kabat-Zinn, Stress Reduction Program, University of Massachusetts Medical Center, 55 Lake Avenue, North, Worcester, MA 01655. *The Stress Reduction and Relaxation Program* is a leading innovator in the integration of meditation into health care and high tension environments such as prisons. For further reading and information contact the above address.

Zen Centre of San Francisco, 300 Page Street, San Francisco, CA 94102, telephone 415 863 3136. Offers a variety of instruction opportunities and retreats in the Soto Zen tradition. Also has a range of affiliated communities and centres.

The centres listed may not have a retreat that suits you but they can be a valuable resource for further contacts. There is a wide variety of publications available for further information. Among these are:

The Buddhist Directory by Peter Lorie and Julie Foakes. Published by Newleaf, an imprint of Macmillan Publishers.

The Good Retreat Guide by Stafford Whiteaker. Published by Rider, an imprint of Random Century Group.

Way of Reincarnation

Judy Hall

Over half the world's population accept reincarnation – they believe they have lived before and will do so again. In the East this is taken for granted, while in the West the belief is rapidly gaining acceptance once again. This comprehensive introduction looks at world thought and contains all the information you need to gain an in-depth knowledge of reincarnation, including:

- *what reincarnation is*
- *its cultural and religious background*
- *how the soul reincarnates*
- *famous people throughout history and their beliefs in reincarnation*
- *the evidence for and against reincarnation.*

Judy Hall is an internationally known author, lecturer and workshop leader and has been a karmic counsellor for 25 years. She has written numerous books on reincarnation and has frequently appeared on radio and television in the UK and US to discuss the subject.

ISBN: 0 00 710290 9

Way of Natural Magic

Nigel Pennick

Natural magic is a way of working with the vital energy around us, including that which comes from our own awareness and intention. Working with natural magic involves simple but powerful practical techniques that anyone can use to bring more magic into their everyday lives. This comprehensive introduction contains all the information you need to gain an in-depth knowledge of magic including:

- *an explanation of earth, mineral, and plant magic*
- *magic animals and how we can work with them*
- *the power within – the magic of the human body*
- *the magic of the land, of food and drink*
- *natural magic charms, talismans and amulets – what they are and how to make and empower them.*

Nigel Pennick has conducted research on ancient monuments, folk traditions, geomancy and magic for over 25 years. In 1975 he founded the Institute of Geomantic Research. He has worked all over Europe, Canada and the US and is a leading author in this field.

ISBN: 0 7225 4038 8

Way of Tibetan Buddhism

Lama Jampa Thaye

Buddhism is now one of the fastest-growing spiritual practices in the West. Tibetan Buddhism is a branch of Buddhism that places particular emphasis on the teacher–disciple relationship which lies at the heart of the spiritual life. This comprehensive introduction contains all the information you need to gain an in-depth knowledge of Tibetan Buddhism, including:

- *what Tibetan Buddhism is and how it developed*
- *an insight into all the basic teachings including Indian, Tibetan and Western practice*
- *the historical background to Buddhism*
- *a summary of the major schools.*

Lama Jampa Thaye (David Stott) is a lecturer in the Religions and Theology Department of Manchester University and a Vajrayana teacher in the Sakya and Kagyu Buddhist traditions, having studied under various masters for over three decades. He is the principal disciple of Karma Thinley Rinpoche, the Director of the Dechen Community in Europe, and the author of a number of books on Buddhism.

ISBN: 0 7225 4017 5

Way of Crystal Healing

Ronald Bonewitz

From one of the world's leading crystal experts, this is the best introduction available for an easy-to-read and sensible beginners guide
to crystals. As well as giving a thorough introduction to the properties and qualities of crystals, this book explores how crystal healing
works, and how it can be combined with related therapies such as
acupuncture, chakra work and energy healing.

The book stands out for its very grounded, realistic approach. The
author believes that many properties are attributed to crystals that
they simply can't have, and that much of the information available
to the public comes from misinformed sources. This book will give
the beginner an honest understanding of the real value of crystals
and of how they can develop their personal experiences of working
with them.

Ronald Bonewitz originally trained as a geologist specializing in
crystal chemistry, and now holds a PhD in Behavioural Science,
emphasizing physiological pyschology. With a reputation for clarity
and integrity, he has given hundreds of crystal courses worldwide
and has written several books on crystals.

ISBN: 0 00 710392 1